MW00987700

4-

AT THE S

Genesis Made

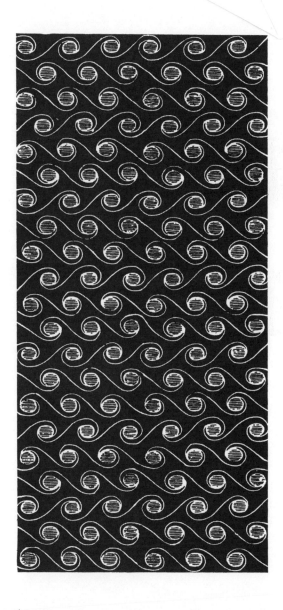

AT THE START

Genesis Made New

A TRANSLATION OF THE HEBREW TEXT

by

Mary Phil Korsak

Foreword by

David Moody

DOUBLEDAY

NEW YORK   LONDON   TORONTO   SYDNEY   AUCKLAND

PUBLISHED BY DOUBLEDAY
a division of Bantam Doubleday Dell Publishing Group, Inc.
1540 Broadway, New York, New York 10036

DOUBLEDAY and the portrayal of an anchor with a dolphin are
trademarks of Doubleday, a division of
Bantam Doubleday Dell Publishing Group, Inc.

Book design by Terry Karydes

Library of Congress Cataloging-in-Publication Data:

Bible. O.T. Genesis. English. Korsak. 1993.
At the start : Genesis made new /
Mary Phil Korsak.
— 1st ed.
p.   cm.
I. Korsak, Mary Phil. II. Title.
BS1233.K67   1993
222′.1105209—dc20   93-916
CIP

Originally published in Belgium in 1992
by the European Association for the
Promotion of Poetry

ISBN 0-385-47180-7
Printed in the United States of America
October 1993

First Edition in the United States of America

1   3   5   7   9   10   8   6   4   2

To

Reverend Jean Mouson (†)

Jean Radermakers S.J.

Armand Abécassis, philosopher, pharisee,

who led the way along the path of biblical studies

TABLE OF CONTENTS

CONTENTS

ACKNOWLEDGMENTS

I wish to recognize my debt to André Chouraqui, who in 1982 suggested that I undertake the task of retranslating Genesis. His French translation was my first guide and his encouragement was unfailing during the progress of this work.

Special gratitude goes to my husband, Léonid Korsak, for so generously facilitating this and every project I have undertaken, and to David Moody (York University, U.K.), who twice perused the manuscript with care, heartening the translator and proposing detailed and discerning criticism of the text. My brother, Philip Malone, was the first to enthuse about the undertaking and his love of his mother tongue inspired many helpful suggestions about the English wording.

My approach to biblical translation has been influenced by the example of Soeur Jeanne D'Arc O.P., the French biblical scholar and translator. A close collaborator of André Chouraqui, she developed an autonomous style in her own French version of the Greek texts of the Gospels. The beauty and clarity of her work seemed to light my way forward. I twice had the privilege of spending some days with her in the Massif Central, in France; despite a terminal illness, the acuteness of her vision was impressive.

Philip Davies (Sheffield University, U.K.) was the first Hebrew scholar from the academic world to approve the project. Philip introduced me to the "Society of Biblical Literature." At its "International Meetings" there were opportunities to meet specialists like Athalya Brenner (Haifa University, Israel), Duane Christensen (Berkeley Institute of Bible, Archaeology and Law, U.S.A.), Mirja and Halvor Ronning (Institute of Holyland Studies, Israel), and Ellen Van Wolde (Tilburg University, Holland).

I would like to express particularly warm thanks to Athalya. Not only did she give time to reading and commenting on the translation but she helped me to develop an awareness of the limitations of androcentric interpretations. Her invitation to speak in a new feminist session at the "Society of Biblical Literature" meeting in Rome, in 1991, prodded me to revise my work at a time when my belief in it was flagging. Duane's enthusiasm was extremely supportive: together we discussed the poetic aspects of biblical texts. It was exciting to meet Mirja, who had just completed her Finnish version of Genesis. We found we understood each other without explanation, as we had followed the same working method. Talking with the Ronnings about rhythm, layout, and the best naming system was most helpful. Ellen kindly read the final version of the first chapters, on which she is expert. I thank her for her encouragement and comments.

There are many other friends and scholars to thank, among them Elisabeth Lacelle (Ottawa University, Canada). I remember with particular pleasure our discussion over lunch in Brussels and the helpful comments she made about the meaning of the Hebrew word *adam*.

On the technical side, my friend Pierre Van Deuren was a painstaking collaborator: we spent hours in front of his computer and it was never too much trouble to redo a page for the sake of a comma. Also, I wish to thank Eugène Van Itterbeek (director), Tony Solomone, Frank Despriet, and Erik Derycke of the European Poetry House (Louvain, Belgium), who, each in a different way, contributed to promoting the first edition.

Finally, I am very grateful to American friends, writer Gertrud Nelson and Publisher Thomas Cahill, for believing in the book and for creating the possibility of wider readership.

FOREWORD

Genesis Made New

Genesis has been the key word for this book of origins ever since it was first translated from the Hebrew into Greek. It could remain *Genesis,* when it was translated from the Greek into Latin, because the word had already entered into that language, as part of the whole family of words from the root γ ε ν ο ς (Lat. *genus*). Moreover, it could thus signify not just the beginning of the world, but the generation of a distinct race; and very aptly so, since the book is really concerned to establish the origins of the people of YHWH.

In English, however, though the word may retain some suggestion of the genesis of the race, in practice it has become little more than a label and a handle: a means of referring to the book, not a way into it. It can be used as unthinkingly as the collective title, *The Bible.* When did it become simply *The Book,* as if there could be no other book in question, no other history? How did *Genesis* come to be read as a record of the origin of the human race, rather than of the Jewish nation? What has happened to this key word can stand for what has happened to the book as a whole. The English tradition of translation, which is of course also a tradition of Christian interpretation, has appropriated this book of YHWH's people and made it all-too familiar, while effacing much of its distinctive character.

The hallowed King James version with its antique splendours represents one kind of familiarity; and there are thoroughly modern versions which represent another kind. Both fail to convey the essential remoteness of the ethos of YHWH and his people from the English-speaking world of today. We need a version which will bring home to us its distance and difference, and so enable us to find a valid relation to it as readers from another time, another world.

Mary Phil Korsak now meets that need with a translation that is radical, scholarly, and brilliantly effective. She has gone back to the Hebrew roots of the text, to recover the roots of the individual words, and to recover also the basic structures of its grammar and syntax and of its narratives. In the Hebrew there are no abstractions. Every word has a distinct triconsonantal root which roots it in a definite object or action. Again, as this is a text rooted in oral performance, its structures are characteristically direct, simple and clear.

> Elohim said
> Let the earth grow grass
> plants seeding seed
> fruit-tree making fruit of its kind
> with its seed in it on the earth
> It was so
> The earth brought forth grass
> plants seeding seed of their kind
> and tree making fruit with its seed in it of its kind
> Elohim saw   How good!

A modern stylist would avoid such repetitions, but the Hebrew delights in them, not for their own sake, but for the way in which they reveal a close-woven texture and pattern in things. With that there is a pleasure in the dramatic structure of the event, a structure which is here clarified and heightened by the laying out of the sequence of phrases for the eye and the ear to take in. There is an unforced and yet strong rhythm, arising naturally from the economy of each line; and then, on a larger scale, from the unfolding shape of the action. The overall effect is of a world seen and understood with powerful immediacy, but by a mind which interprets its experience with a difference. The great virtue of Mary Phil Korsak's version is to have caught that difference.

She has achieved the necessary double perspective—bringing home what yet remains remote—by practising a double fidelity. Her translation is true to the English language, and yet it is in an English modified and refined by the characteristic qualities of the Hebrew original. It nowhere departs from what can properly and naturally be said in modern English. But if, as will often be the case, current usage would be likely to put it another way, then the point of difference will be precisely the point of the live contact between the mind of a modern reader and the primal Hebrew mentality.

Any fresh revelation, whatever its source, must be experienced before it can be understood, for it is always what has been experienced that is to be understood. This translation offers a new experience of the book hitherto known as *Genesis,* and it offers through that the possibility of a new understanding of it. It makes the book, for me at least, more mystifying and more absorbing; less to do with God's ways than with a nation's visions and revisions of its history; more polemical, and more authentic as a record of a specific culture; more dramatic; and more revelatory of the mind and motives of the people of YHWH. As T. S. Eliot said that Ezra Pound was the inventor of Chinese poetry for our time, so it can now be said that Mary Phil Korsak has invented the first book of the Bible for the contemporary English-speaking world.

8 IX 91   A.D. MOODY

CHAPTER 1

1   At the start Elohim created the skies and the earth

2   —the earth was tohu-bohu
darkness on the face of the deep
and the breath of Elohim
hovering on the face of the waters—

3   Elohim said
Let light be
Light was
4   Elohim saw the light How good!
Elohim separated the light from the darkness
5   Elohim called to the light "Day"
To the darkness he called "Night"
It was evening, it was morning
One day

6   Elohim said
Let a vault be in the middle of the waters
it shall separate waters from waters
7   Elohim made the vault
It separated the waters under the vault
from the waters above the vault
It was so
8   Elohim called to the vault "Skies"

1 Elohim. See Translator's Postscript. Others: God.

It was evening, it was morning
A second day

9 Elohim said
   Let the waters under the skies be massed to one place
   Let the dry be seen
   It was so
10 Elohim called to the dry "Earth"
   To the massing of the waters he called "Seas"
   Elohim saw. How good!
11 Elohim said
   Let the earth grow grass
   plants seeding seed
   fruit-tree making fruit of its kind
   with its seed in it on the earth
   It was so
12 The earth brought forth grass
   plants seeding seed of their kind
   and tree making fruit with its seed in it of its kind
   Elohim saw How good!
13 It was evening, it was morning
   A third day

14 Elohim said
   Let lights be in the vault of the skies
   to separate the day from the night
   They shall be signs for set times, for days and years
15 They shall be lights in the vault of the skies
   to light upon the earth
   It was so
16 Elohim made the two great lights
   the great light for ruling the day

the small light for ruling the night
and the stars

17 Elohim gave them to the vault of the skies
to light upon the earth

18 to rule the day and the night
and to separate the light from the darkness
Elohim saw How good!

19 It was evening, it was morning
A fourth day

20 Elohim said
Let the waters swarm with a swarm of living souls
and let fowl fly above the earth
upon the face of the vault of the skies

21 Elohim created the great monsters
all living souls that creep
with which the waters swarm of their kind
and every winged fowl of its kind
Elohim saw How good!

22 Elohim blessed them, saying
Be fruitful, increase, fill the waters in the seas
Let the fowl increase on the earth

23 It was evening, it was morning
A fifth day

24 Elohim said
Let the earth bring forth living souls of their kind
cattle, creeper and beast of the earth of its kind
It was so

25 Elohim made the beast of the earth of its kind
the cattle of their kind
and every creeper of the ground of its kind
Elohim saw How good!

26   Elohim said
    We will make a groundling (Adam)
    in our image, after our likeness
    Let them govern the fish of the sea
    the fowl of the skies, the cattle, all the earth
    every creeper that creeps on the earth

27   Elohim created the groundling in his image
    created it in the image of Elohim
    male and female created them

28   Elohim blessed them
    Elohim said to them
    Be fruitful, increase, fill the earth, subject it
    Govern the fish of the sea, the fowl of the skies
    every beast that creeps on the earth

29   Elohim said, Here I give you
    all plants seeding seed upon the face of all the earth
    and every tree with tree-fruit in it seeding seed
    It shall be for you for eating

30   And for every beast of the earth
    for every fowl of the skies
    for all that creeps on the earth with living soul in it
    all green of plants for eating
    It was so

31   Elohim saw all he had made Here! it was very good
    It was evening, it was morning
    The sixth day

CHAPTER 2

1 They were finished, the skies, the earth
and all their company
2 Elohim had finished on the seventh day
his work that he had done
He ceased on the seventh day
from all his work that he had done
3 Elohim blessed the seventh day and made it holy
for on it he ceased from all his work
that Elohim had created and done

4 These are the breedings of the skies and the earth
at their creation

On the day YHWH Elohim made earth and skies
5 no shrub of the field was yet in the earth
no plant of the field had yet sprouted
for YHWH Elohim had not made it rain on the earth
and there was no groundling to serve the ground
6 But a surge went up from the earth
and gave drink to all the face of the ground
7 YHWH Elohim formed the groundling, soil of the ground
He blew into its nostrils the blast of life
and the groundling became a living soul

8 YHWH Elohim planted a garden in Eden in the east
There he set the groundling he had formed

---

4 YHWH: the personal name of the God of the Hebrews is not pronounced.
Read Adonai, or Yahweh, or the Lord.

9   YHWH Elohim made sprout from the ground
       all trees attractive to see and good for eating
       the tree of life in the middle of the garden
       and the tree of the knowing of good and bad

10   A river goes out in Eden to give drink to the garden
       From there it divides and becomes four heads
11   The name of the first is Pishon
       It winds through all the land of Havilah
       where there is gold
12   The gold of that land is good
       Bdellium is there and onyx stone
13   The name of the second river is Gihon
       It winds through all the land of Cush
14   The name of the third river is Tigris
       It goes east of Asshur
       The fourth river is Euphrates

15   YHWH Elohim took the groundling
       and set it to rest in the garden of Eden
       to serve it and keep it
16   YHWH Elohim commanded the groundling, saying
       Of every tree of the garden eat! you shall eat
17   but of the tree of the knowing of good and bad
       you shall not eat
       for on the day you eat of it
       die! you shall die

18   YHWH Elohim said
       It is not good for the groundling to be alone
       I will make for it a help as its counterpart

12 onyx: meaning of Hebrew uncertain.

6

19   YHWH Elohim formed out of the ground
     all beasts of the field, all fowl of the skies
     and brought them to the groundling
     to see what it would call them
     Whatever the groundling called to each living soul
     that is its name
20   The groundling called names for all the cattle
     for all fowl of the skies, for all beasts of the field
     But for a groundling it found no help as its counterpart
21   YHWH Elohim made a swoon fall upon the groundling
     it slept
     He took one of its sides
     and closed up the flesh in its place
22   YHWH Elohim built the side
     he had taken from the groundling into woman
     He brought her to the groundling
23   The groundling said
         This one this time
         is bone from my bones
         flesh from my flesh
         This one shall be called wo-man
         for from man
         she has been taken this one

24   So a man will leave his father and his mother
     he will cling to his wo-man
     and they will become one flesh

25   The two of them were naked
     the groundling and his woman
     they were not ashamed

CHAPTER 3

1 The serpent was the most shrewd
of all the beasts of the field
that YHWH Elohim had made
It said to the woman, So Elohim said
You shall not eat of all the trees of the garden . . .

2 The woman said to the serpent
We will eat the fruit of the trees of the garden

3 but of the fruit of the tree
in the middle of the garden, Elohim said
You shall not eat of it, you shall not touch it
lest you die

4 The serpent said to the woman
Die! you shall not die

5 No, Elohim knows that the day you eat of it
your eyes will be opened
and you will be as Elohim knowing good and bad

6 The woman saw that the tree was good for eating
yes, an allurement to the eyes
and that the tree was attractive to get insight
She took of its fruit and ate
She also gave to her man with her and he ate

7 The eyes of the two of them were opened
they knew that they were naked
They sewed fig leaves together
and made themselves loinclothes

8 They heard the voice of YHWH Elohim
walking in the garden in the breeze of the day

The groundling and his woman hid from YHWH Elohim
in the middle of the tree of the garden

9   YHWH Elohim called to the groundling and said to him
    Where are you?
10 He said, I heard your voice in the garden
    and I was afraid for I was naked
    and I hid
11 He said, Who told you that you were naked?
    Did you eat of the tree
    I commanded you not to eat of?
12 The groundling said
    The woman you gave to be with me,
    she, she gave me of the tree and I ate
13 YHWH Elohim said to the woman
    What have you done?
    The woman said
    The serpent enticed me and I ate

14 YHWH Elohim said to the serpent
        As you have done this
        you are banned from all the cattle
        of all the beasts of the field
        You shall go on your stomach
        and you shall eat soil
        all the days of your life
15   I will put enmity between you and the woman
        between your seed and her seed
        It, it shall strike at your head
        and you, you shall strike at its heel

16 To the woman he said
        Increase! I will increase

your pains and your conceivings
With pains you shall breed sons
For your man your longing
and he, he shall rule you

17 To the groundling he said
As you have heard your woman's voice
and have eaten of the tree
of which I commanded you, saying
You shall not eat of it!
cursed is the ground for you
With pains you shall eat of it
all the days of your life

18 Thorn and thistle it shall sprout for you
You shall eat the plants of the field

19 With the sweat of your face you shall eat bread
till you return to the ground
for from it you were taken
for soil you are and to the soil you shall return

20 The groundling called his woman's name Life (Eve)
for she is the mother of all that lives

21 YHWH Elohim made for the groundling and his woman
robes of skin and clothed them

22 YHWH Elohim said
Here, the groundling has become as one of us
knowing good and bad
Now, let it not put out its hand
to take from the tree of life also
and eat and live for ever!

23 YHWH Elohim sent it away from the garden of Eden
to serve the ground from which it was taken

24   He cast out the groundling
      and made dwell east of the garden of Eden
      the Cherubim and the scorching, turning sword
      to keep the road to the tree of life

CHAPTER 4

1 The groundling knew his woman Eve
  She conceived and bred Acquisition (Cain)
  She said, I have acquired a man with YHWH
2 Once more she bred, his brother Abel
  Abel became a shepherd of flocks
  Cain was a servant of the ground

3 At the end of days
  Cain brought fruit of the ground
  a present for YHWH
4 Abel also brought firstlings of his flock
  with their fat
  YHWH regarded Abel and his present
5 but Cain and his present he did not regard
  This inflamed Cain much, his face fell
6 YHWH said to Cain
        Why does this inflame you?
        Why has your face fallen?
7   Surely, if you do good
        you will lift up
        If you do not do good
        at the entrance sin is crouching
        for you it's longing
        and you, you shall rule it

8 Cain said to his brother Abel . . .
  And when they were in the field

7 Hebrew verse obscure.

Cain rose up against his brother Abel
and killed him

9   YHWH said to Cain, Where is your brother Abel?
He said, I do not know
Am I a keeper for my brother?

10   He said, What have you done?
The voice of your brother's blood
cries to me from the ground

11   Now you are banned from the ground
whose mouth has gaped
to take your brother's blood from your hand

12   When you serve the ground
it shall no more give its force to you
Wavering and wandering you shall be on the earth

13   Cain said to YHWH
My punishment is too great to bear

14   Here you have cast me out this day
from the face of the ground
I shall be concealed from your face
I shall be wavering and wandering on the earth
and whoever finds me will kill me

15   YHWH said to him, For sure, whoever kills Cain
shall suffer vengeance 7 times
YHWH set a sign on Cain
so that whoever found him would not strike him

16   Cain went out from the face of YHWH
and settled in the land of Wandering (Nod)
east of Eden

17   Cain knew his woman
She conceived and bred Enoch

He built a town and called the name of the town
like the name of his son, Enoch

18   For Enoch was bred Irad
Irad bred Mehujael
Mehujael bred Methusael
Methusael bred Lamech

19   Lamech took two women
The name of the first was Adah
the name of the second, Zillah

20   Adah bred Jabal
He was the father
of those who sit amidst tent and live-stock

21   His brother's name was Jubal
He was the father of all who hold the lyre and pipe

22   Zillah also bred, Tubal-Cain
forger of all, craftsman in bronze and iron
and Tubal-Cain's sister, Naamah

23   Lamech said to his women
      Adah and Zillah, hear my voice
      Women of Lamech, give ear to my say
      For I have killed a man for wounding me
      a child for bruising me

24   For 7 times is Cain avenged
      but Lamech 77 times

25   Adam knew his woman again
She bred a son
She called his name Seth

18 Mehujael bred. Hebrew: Mehijael bred.

"for Elohim has set another seed in Abel's place
yes, Cain killed him"
26 A son was bred for Seth also
He called his name Enosh

Then they began to call upon the name of YHWH

CHAPTER 5

1 This is the record of the breedings of Adam

—on the day Elohim created a groundling
in the likeness of Elohim he made it
2 male and female created them
and blessed them
and called their name Groundling (Adam)
on the day of their creation—

3 Adam lived 130 years
and bred in his likeness, after his image
He called his name Seth
4 The days of Adam after he bred Seth were 800 years
He bred sons and daughters
5 All the days Adam lived were 930 years, then he died

6 Seth lived 105 years and bred Enosh
7 Seth lived after he bred Enosh 807 years
He bred sons and daughters
8 All the days of Seth were 912 years, then he died

9 Enosh lived 90 years and bred Kenan
10 Enosh lived after he bred Kenan 815 years
He bred sons and daughters
11 All the days of Enosh were 905 years, then he died

12 Kenan lived 70 years and bred Mahalalel

13   Kenan lived after he bred Mahalalel 840 years
       He bred sons and daughters
14   All the days of Kenan were 910 years, then he died

15   Mahalalel lived 65 years and bred Jared
16   Mahalalel lived after he bred Jared 830 years
       He bred sons and daughters
17   All the days of Mahalalel were 895 years, then he died
18   Jared lived 162 years and bred Enoch
19   Jared lived after he bred Enoch 800 years
       He bred sons and daughters
20   All the days of Jared were 962 years, then he died

21   Enoch lived 65 years and bred Methuselah
22   Enoch walked with the Elohim after he bred Methuselah
          300 years
       He bred sons and daughters
23   All the days of Enoch were 365 years
24   Enoch walked with the Elohim, then he was no more
       for Elohim took him

25   Methuselah lived 187 years and bred Lamech
26   Methuselah lived after he bred Lamech 782 years
       He bred sons and daughters
27   All the days of Methuselah were 969 years, then he died

28   Lamech lived 182 years and bred a son
29   He called his name Rest (Noah), saying
       This one will bring us comfort from our doing
       and from the pains of our hands
       out of the ground YHWH has cursed
30   Lamech lived after he bred Noah 595 years
       He bred sons and daughters

31   All the days of Lamech were 777 years, then he died

32   Noah was 500 years old
      and Noah bred Shem, Ham, and Japheth

CHAPTER 6

1 When the groundling began to increase
on the face of the ground
and daughters were bred for them

2 the sons of the Elohim saw the daughters of the groundling
How beautiful they were!
They took themselves women from any they chose

3 YHWH said
My breath shall not stay in the groundling for ever
since it is but flesh
Its days shall be a hundred and twenty years

4 The giants were on earth in those days
and after that also when the sons of the Elohim came in
to the daughters of the groundling
and they bred for them
Those were the mighty who were of old
the men of name

5 YHWH saw
that the groundling's badness increased on earth
All the thoughts its heart formed were only bad
all the day long

6 YHWH was sorry he had made the groundling on earth
he was pained in his heart

7 YHWH said
I will blot out the groundling I have created

3 stay: meaning of Hebrew uncertain.

from the face of the ground
from groundling to cattle, to creeper
and to fowl of the skies
for I am sorry that I made them

8   But Noah found favour in YHWH's eyes

9   These are the breedings of Noah
Noah was a just man, wholesome in that age
He walked with the Elohim, Noah

10   Noah bred three sons, Shem, Ham and Japheth

11   The earth had been destroyed before the Elohim
the earth was filled with violence

12   Elohim saw the earth Here! it had been destroyed
for all flesh had destroyed its road on earth

13   Elohim said to Noah
The end of all flesh has come before me
for the earth is full of violence because of them
Here I am, I will destroy them with the earth

14   Make yourself an ark of cypress-wood
You shall make the ark with compartments
Asphalt it inside and outside with asphalt

15   Thus you shall make it
three hundred cubits, the length of the ark
fifty cubits, its breadth
thirty cubits, its height

16   You shall make a skylight for the ark
and finish it by a cubit up above
You shall set the entrance of the ark in its flank
You shall make bottom, second and third decks

17   And I, I am here
bringing the flood, waters upon the earth

16 First sentence: Hebrew obscure

to destroy all flesh with breath of life in it
under the skies
Everything on earth shall pass away

18   But I will set up my pact with you
you shall come into the ark, you
your sons, your woman and your sons' women with you

19   Of all that lives, of all flesh
you shall bring two of each into the ark
to preserve life with you
they shall be male and female

20   Of the fowl of their kind, of the cattle of their kind
and of all that creeps on the ground of its kind
two of each shall come in to you to preserve life

21   And you, take for yourself of all eatables that are eaten
Gather it to you
It shall be for you and for them for eating

22   Noah did all that Elohim commanded him
He did so

CHAPTER 7

1   YHWH said to Noah
Come, you and all your household, into the ark
for I have seen you are just
before me in this age
2   Of all clean beasts you shall take seven and seven
a man and its woman
and of beasts that are not clean, two
a man and its woman
3   also of the fowl of the skies, seven and seven
male and female
to preserve seed alive on the face of all the earth
4   For in seven days, I, I will make it rain upon the earth
forty days and forty nights
I will blot out all existence I have made
from the face of the ground
5   Noah did all that YHWH commanded him

6   Noah was six hundred years old and the flood came
waters upon the earth
7   Noah came, his sons, his woman
and his sons' women with him into the ark
because of the waters of the flood
8   Of the clean beasts and the beasts that are not clean
of the fowl and all that creeps on the ground
9   two and two, they came in to Noah into the ark
male and female
as Elohim had commanded Noah

10   There were seven days
and the waters of the flood were upon the earth

11   In the year six hundred of Noah's life
in the second month
on the seventeenth of the month
on this day
all the springs of the abundant deep erupted
the floodgates of the skies were opened

12   There was downpour upon the earth
forty days and forty nights

13   On that very day Noah came
Shem, Ham and Japheth, Noah's sons
and Noah's woman and his sons' three women with them
into the ark

14   They and every beast of its kind
all the cattle of their kind
every creeper that creeps on the earth of its kind
all that flies of its kind, all birds, all wing

15   they came in to Noah into the ark
two and two of all flesh with breath of life in it

16   Those coming in, male and female of all flesh, came in
as Elohim had commanded him
YHWH shut him in

17   The flood was upon the earth forty days
The waters increased and lifted the ark
it was raised above the earth

18   The waters grew mighty
they increased much upon the earth
And the ark went upon the face of the waters

19   The waters grew much, much mightier upon the earth
They covered all the high mountains under all the skies

20   Fifteen cubits up above the waters grew mighty
       they had covered the mountains

21   All flesh that crept on the earth passed away
       fowl, cattle, beast
       every swarm that swarmed on the earth
       and every groundling

22   everything with the blast of the breath of life in its nostrils
       everything that was on the dry died

23   He blotted out all existence from the face of the ground
       from groundling to cattle, to creeper
       and to fowl of the skies
       they were blotted out from the earth
       Only Noah remained and those with him in the ark

24   The waters were mighty upon the earth
       a hundred and fifty days

CHAPTER 8

1   Elohim remembered Noah
and all the beasts, all the cattle with him in the ark
Elohim made a breath pass over the earth
the waters abated

2   the springs of the deep
the floodgates of the skies were stopped up
the downpour from the skies was kept back

3   The waters turned from the earth, going and turning
The waters waned
at the end of a hundred and fifty days

4   The ark rested in the seventh month
on the seventeenth day of the month
on the Ararat mountains

5   The waters were going and waning
till the tenth month
In the tenth, on the first of the month
the heads of the mountains were seen

6   At the end of forty days
Noah opened the window of the ark he had made

7   He sent the raven
It went out, going out and turning
until the waters dried upon the earth

8   He sent the dove from him
to see if the waters had lessened
upon the face of the ground

9   The dove did not find rest for the sole of its foot
It returned to him in the ark

for the waters were upon the face of all the earth
He put out his hand
took it and brought it towards him in the ark
10   He waited again seven other days
and once more he sent the dove from the ark
11   The dove came to him at eventide
and here! a fresh olive-leaf was in its mouth
Noah knew that the waters had lessened on the earth
12   He waited again seven other days
He sent the dove
but it returned to him again no more

13   It was year six hundred and one
the first month, the one of the month
the waters were drying upon the earth
Noah put aside the covering of the ark
He saw Here! the face of the ground was drying
14   In the second month
on the twenty-seventh day of the month
the earth was dry

15   Elohim spoke to Noah, saying
16   Go out of the ark, you, your woman, your sons
and your sons' women with you
17   Every beast that is with you of all flesh
fowl, cattle, every creeper that creeps on the earth
bring them out with you
They shall swarm on the earth
they shall be fruitful and increase on the earth
18   Noah went out, his sons, his woman
and his sons' women with him
19   Every beast, every creeper, every fowl

everything that creeps on the earth
clan by clan, they went out of the ark

20 Noah built an altar to YHWH
He took of every clean beast and every clean fowl
and offered up offerings on the altar
21 YHWH smelled the soothing smell
YHWH said in his heart
Nevermore again will I doom the ground
because of the groundling
for what forms in the groundling's heart
is bad from its youth on
but nevermore will I strike all that lives
as I have done
22   All the days the earth lasts
seeding and harvest
cold and heat
summer and winter
day and night
shall not cease

CHAPTER 9

1 Elohim blessed Noah and his sons
   He said to them
   Be fruitful, increase, fill the earth
2 Fear of you, terror of you
   shall be upon all the beasts of the earth
   all the fowl of the skies
   all that creeps on the ground
   all the fish of the sea
   they are given into your hand
3 Every creeper that lives shall be for you for eating
   as the green of plants
   I give all to you
4 Only flesh with its lifeblood in it you shall not eat
5 For your lifeblood I will require a reckoning
   Of the hand of every beast I will require it
   and of the hand of the groundling
   Of the hand of its brother man
   I will require a reckoning for the groundling's life
6 Whoever sheds the blood of the groundling
   by the groundling his blood shall be shed
   for in the image of Elohim he made the groundling
7 But you, be fruitful, increase, swarm on earth
   increase on it

8 Elohim said to Noah and to his sons with him, saying
9 And I, I am here, I set up my pact with you
   with your seed after you
10 with every living soul that is with you

fowl, cattle, every beast of the earth with you
all that went out from the ark
all that lives on the earth

11   I will set up my pact with you
never again shall all flesh be cut off
by the waters of the flood
never again shall there be a flood
to destroy the earth

12   Elohim said, This is the sign of the pact
that I give between me and you
and every living soul with you
for the everlasting ages

13   I give my bow to the cloud
it shall be the sign of the pact
between me and the earth

14   When I cloud the earth with cloud
and the bow in the cloud is seen

15   I will remember my pact between me and you
and every living soul in all flesh
Never again shall the waters become a flood
to destroy all flesh

16   There will be the bow in the cloud
I will see it and remember the everlasting pact
between Elohim and every living soul in all flesh
that is upon the earth

17   Elohim said to Noah
This is the sign of the pact that I have set up
between me and all flesh upon the earth

18   The sons of Noah
going out of the ark were Shem, Ham and Japheth
Ham was the father of Canaan

19 These three were the sons of Noah
  from these all the earth scattered

20 Noah, a man of the ground
  was the first to plant a vineyard
21 He drank of the wine, became drunk
  and uncovered himself in the middle of his tent
22 Ham, the father of Canaan, saw his father's genitals
  He told his brothers outside
23 But Shem and Japheth took the tunic
  the two of them set it on their shoulders
  They went backwards and covered their father's genitals
  Facing the other way
  their father's genitals they did not see

24 Noah woke up from his wine
  He knew what his youngest son had done to him
25 He said
    Cursed is Canaan
    A servant of servants he shall be to his brothers!
26 He said
    Blessed is YHWH Elohim of Shem
    Canaan shall be their servant!
27   Elohim shall enlarge for Enlargement (Japheth)
    he shall dwell in the tents of Shem
    Canaan shall be their servant!

28 Noah lived after the flood 350 years
29 All the days of Noah were 950 years, then he died

CHAPTER 10

1   These are the breedings of Noah's sons
    Shem, Ham and Japheth
    Sons were bred for them after the flood

2   Sons of Japheth
    Gomer, Magog, Madai, Javan, Tubal, Meshech and Tiras
3   Sons of Gomer
    Ashkenaz, Riphath and Togarmah
4   Sons of Javan
    Elishah, Tarshish, the Kittim and the Dodanim
5   From these the coastland nations divided
    in their lands, each with its tongue
    by their clans, within their nations

6   Sons of Ham
    Cush, Mizraim, Put and Canaan
7   Sons of Cush
    Seba, Havilah, Sabtah, Raamah and Sabteca
    Sons of Raamah: Sheba and Dedan
8   Cush bred Nimrod
    he was the first to be mighty on earth
9   He was a mighty hunter before YHWH
    So it is said, Like Nimrod, a mighty hunter before YHWH!
10 The start of his kingdom was Babylon
    Erech, Accad and Calne in the land of Shinar
11 Out of that land went Asshur
    He built Nineveh, Rehobot-ir, Calah
12 and Resen, between Nineveh and Calah the great town

13 Mizraim bred the Ludim
    the Anamim, the Lehabim, the Naphtuhim
14 the Pathrusim and the Casluhim
    and the Caphtorim that the Philistines issued from
15 Canaan bred Sidon his first-born and Heth
16 the Jebusites, the Amorites, the Girgashites
17 the Hivites, the Arkites, the Sinites,
18 the Arvadites, the Zemarites and the Hamathites
    Afterwards, the clans of the Canaanites scattered
19 and the border of the Canaanites was from Sidon
    till you come to Gerar near Gaza
    till Sodom, Gomorrah, Admah and Zeboyim near Lasha
20 These are the sons of Ham
    according to their clans and their tongues
    by their lands and their nations

21 Children were bred for Shem also
    he, the father of all the sons of Eber
    and the elder brother of Japheth
22 Sons of Shem
    Elam, Asshur, Arpachshad, Lud and Aram
23 Sons of Aram
    Us, Hul, Gether and Mash
24 Arpachshad bred Shelah
    Shelah bred Eber
25 For Eber two sons were bred
    the name of the first was Splitting (Peleg)
    for in his days the earth split up
    His brother's name was Joktan
26 Joktan bred Almodad, Sheleph, Hazamarvet, Jerah
27 Hadoram, Uzal, Diklah
28 Obal, Abimael, Sheba

29   Ophir, Havilah and Jabab
      all these were sons of Ioqtan
30   Their settlement was from Meshah
      till you come to Sephar the mountain of the east
31   These are the sons of Shem
      according to their clans and their tongues
      by their lands, according to their nations

32   These are the clans of Noah's sons,
      according to their breedings, within their nations
      From these the nations divided on earth
      after the flood

CHAPTER 11

1   All the earth had one lip, one speech
2   When they set out from the east
    they found a dale in the land of Shinar
    and settled there
3   They said, each to his companion
    Come, let us brick bricks!
    Let us burn them in a burning!
    For them brick was stone, bitumen was clay for them
4   They said, Come, let us build ourselves a town and a tower
    with its head in the skies
    let us make ourselves a name
    else we shall be scattered
    upon the face of all the earth

5   YHWH went down to see the town and the tower
    the sons of the groundling had built
6   YHWH said, Here is one people, one lip for them all!
    They have begun to do this
    and now nothing will check them
    in all that they plan to do!
7   Come, we will go down and make their lip babble there
    so that no man shall hear the lip of his companion
8   YHWH scattered them from there
    upon the face of all the earth
    They stopped building the town
9   So they called its name Babel
    for there YHWH made the lip of all the earth babble

and from there YHWH scattered them
upon the face of all the earth

10 These are the breedings of Shem

Shem was 100 years old and he bred Arpachshad
two years after the flood
11 Shem lived after he bred Arpachshad 500 years
He bred sons and daughters

12 Arpachshad lived 35 years and bred Shelah
13 Arpachshad lived after he bred Shelah 403 years
He bred sons and daughters

14 Shelah lived 30 years and bred Eber
15 Shelah lived after he bred Eber 403 years
He bred sons and daughters

16 Eber lived 34 years and bred Peleg
17 Eber lived after he bred Peleg 430 years
He bred sons and daughters

18 Peleg lived 30 years and bred Reu
19 Peleg lived after he bred Reu 209 years
He bred sons and daughters

20 Reu lived 32 years and bred Serug
21 Reu lived after he bred Serug 207 years
He bred sons and daughters

22 Serug lived 30 years and bred Nahor
23 Serug lived after he bred Nahor 200 years
He bred sons and daughters

24 Nahor lived 29 years and bred Terah
25 Nahor lived after he bred Terah 119 years
He bred sons and daughters

26 Terah lived 70 years
He bred Abram, Nahor and Haran

27 These are the breedings of Terah
Terah bred Abram, Nahor and Haran
Haran bred Lot

28 Haran died facing his father Terah
in the land of his kin at Ur of the Chaldeans
29 Abram and Nahor took themselves women
The name of Abram's woman was Sarai
The name of Nahor's woman was Milcah
daughter of Haran
the father of Milcah and the father of Iscah
30 Sarai was barren
For her no childling

31 Terah took his son Abram
and his son's son, Lot son of Haran
and his daughter-in-law Sarai, his son Abram's woman
He went out with them from Ur of the Chaldeans
to go to the land of Canaan
They came to Haran and settled there
32 The days of Terah were 205 years
Terah died in Haran

CHAPTER 12

1 YHWH said to Abram
   Go from your land, from your kin
   and from your father's house
   to the land that I will let you see
2 I will make you into a great nation
   I will bless you
   I will make your name great
   Be a blessing
3 I will bless those who bless you
   he who dooms you I will curse
   Through you shall be blessed
   all the clans of the ground

4 Abram went as YHWH had spoken to him
   Lot went with him
   Abram was seventy-five years old
   when he went out from Haran
5 Abram took his woman Sarai, his brother's son Lot
   all their gain they had gained
   and the souls they had made in Haran
   They went out to go to the land of Canaan
   They came into the land of Canaan
6 Abram passed through the land
   to the place at Shechem, to the Oak of More
   The Canaanites were then in the land

7 YHWH was seen by Abram
   He said, To your seed I will give this land

He built an altar there
to YHWH who had been seen by him
8   He moved on from there to the mountain east of Bethel
He spread his tent
with Bethel seawards and Ai to the east
He built an altar there to YHWH
and called upon the name of YHWH
9   Abram set out stage by stage for the Negeb
10 There was hunger in the land
Abram went down to Egypt to sojourn there
for the hunger was heavy in the land
11 When he came near to Egypt
he said to his woman Sarai
Look! I know that you are a woman fair to see
12 When the Egyptians see you
they will say, This is his woman
They will kill me but let you live!
13 Please say that you are my sister
so that it will go well with me because of you
and my soul will live thanks to you

14 When Abram came into Egypt
the Egyptians saw the woman
yes, she was very fair!
15 The princes of Pharaoh saw her
they praised her to Pharaoh
The woman was taken into Pharaoh's household
16 It was well with Abram because of her
for him, flocks, herds, asses
servants, maids, she-asses and camels

17 But YHWH smote Pharaoh with great smites

and his household
on account of Abram's woman Sarai
18   Pharaoh called Abram and said
What have you done to me?
Why did you not tell me that she was your woman?
19   Why did you say, She is my sister?
I took her for my woman
Now, here is your woman!
Take her and go!

20   Pharaoh put men in command over him
they sent him away with his woman and all he had

CHAPTER 13

1   Abram went up from Egypt, he, his woman, all he had
    and Lot with him, to the Negeb
2   Abram was heavy with live-stock, silver and gold
3   He went by stages from the Negeb to Bethel
    to the place where his tent had been at the beginning
    between Bethel and Ai
4   to the place where he had first made the altar
    There Abram called upon the name of YHWH

5   Lot also, who went with Abram
    had flocks, herds and tents
6   But the land could not bear them to settle together
    their gain was so abundant
    they were not able to settle together
7   There was a quarrel
    between the herdsmen of Abram's live-stock
    and the herdsmen of Lot's live-stock
    The Canaanites and the Perizzites
    were then settled in the land

8   Abram said to Lot
    Let there be no quarrelling between me and you
    between my herdsmen and your herdsmen
    for we are brother-men
9   Is not all the land before you?
    Please separate from me
    if to the left, I will go to the right
    if to the right, I will go to the left

10 Lot lifted up his eyes
    He saw all the circuit of the Jordan
    yes, it was all given drink
    —before YHWH destroyed Sodom and Gomorrah
    it was like YHWH's garden, like the land of Egypt—
    till you come to Zoar
11 Lot chose for himself all the circuit of the Jordan
    Lot set out eastwards
    They separated, each man from his brother
12 Abram settled in the land of Canaan
    and Lot settled in the towns of the circuit
    he moved his tent as far as Sodom
13 But the men of Sodom were bad
    they sinned much against YHWH

14 YHWH said to Abram
    after Lot had separated from him
    Lift up your eyes and see
    from the place where you are
    to the north, to the Negeb, to the east, to the sea
15 for all the land that you see I give to you
    and to your seed for ever
16 I will make your seed like the soil of the earth
    if a man was able to number the soil of the earth
    your seed also could be numbered
17 Rise and walk in the land
    through its length and through its breadth
    for I give it to you

18 Abram moved his tent
    he came and settled by the Oaks of Mamre
    which are at Hebron
    There he built an altar to YHWH

CHAPTER 14

1   In the days of Amraphel king of Shinar
Arioch king of Ellasar, Chedorlaomer king of Elam
and Tidal king of Goiim

2   They made war on Bera king of Sodom
Birsha king of Gomorrah, Shinab king of Admah
Shemeber king of Zeboiim
and the king of Bela—that is Zoar

3   All these joined in the Valley of Siddim
—that is the Salt Sea

4   Twelve years they had served Chedorlaomer
but in the thirteenth year they had rebelled

5   In the fourteenth year
Chedorlaomer came and the kings with him
They struck the Rephaim in Ashteroth-karnaim
the Zuzim in Ham, the Emim in Shaveh-kiriathaim

6   and the Horites in their mountains of Seir
as far as El-paran, which is near the wilderness

7   They turned back and came to En-mishpat
—that is Kadesh
They struck all the country of the Amalekites
and also the Amorites
who were settled in Hazazon-tamar

8   The king of Sodom went out and the king of Gomorrah
the king of Admah, the king of Zeboiim
and the king of Bela—that is Zoar
and they lined up for war with them
in the Valley of Siddim

9   with Chedorlaomer king of Elam, Tidal king of Goiim

Amraphel king of Shinar and Arioch king of Ellasar
—four kings against five!

10 The Valley of Siddim! Wells, wells of bitumen!
The kings of Sodom and Gomorrah fled and fell there
and the remainder fled to the mountain
11 They took all the gain of Sodom and Gomorrah
and all their food and went away
12 They took Lot with his gain
—the son of Abram's brother—and went away
He had settled in Sodom

13 The one who escaped came and told Abram the Hebrew
He was dwelling at the Oaks of Mamre the Amorite
brother of Eshkol and brother of Aner
who were members of Abram's pact
14 When Abram heard that his brother had been captured
he drew out his retainers bred in his household
three hundred and eighteen
and pursued as far as Dan
15 He deployed against them at night
he and his servants
He struck and pursued as far as Hobah
which is to the left of Damascus
16 He returned all the gain
He also returned his brother Lot and his gain
also the women and the people

17 On his return from striking Chedorlaomer
and the kings with him

14 retainers: meaning of Hebrew uncertain.

the king of Sodom went out to greet him
in the Valley of Shaveh—that is the King's Valley

18 Melchizedek king of Salem brought out bread and wine
He was a priest of El Elyon
19 He blessed him and said
Blessed is Abram by El Elyon
founder of skies and earth!
20 Blessed is El Elyon
who has delivered your oppressors into your hand!
He gave him a tenth of everything
21 The king of Sodom said to Abram
Give me the souls
The gain take for yourself
22 Abram said to the king of Sodom
I raise my hand to YHWH El Elyon
founder of skies and earth
23 Not a thread, not a sandal-strap
will I take of all that is yours
You shall not say, I, I enriched Abram!
24 Nothing for me! Only what the youths ate
and the share of the men who went with me
Aner, Eshkol and Mamre
they shall take their share

18 El Elyon. Others: God Most High

CHAPTER 15

1 After these things YHWH's word came to Abram
   in a vision, saying,
   Do not be afraid, Abram
   I am your shield
   Your hire shall be very abundant
2 Abram said, My Lord YHWH, what can you give me
   when I go childless
   and the successor to my house is Eliezer of Damascus?
3 Abram said, Here, to me you have given no seed!
   Here, one born in my household will be my heir!
4 But here YHWH's word came to him, saying
   That one shall not be your heir
   but he who issues from your belly
   he shall be your heir
5 He brought him outside and said
   Look at the skies and count the stars
   if you are able to count them!
   He said to him, Thus shall your seed be
6 He trusted in YHWH, who thought it justness in him

7 He said to him
   I, YHWH
   who brought you out of Ur of the Chaldeans
   to give you this land to inherit it

8 But he said, My Lord YHWH
   how shall I know I will inherit it?

---

2 Last line: meaning of Hebrew uncertain.

9   He said to him, Bring me a three-year-old heifer
     a three-year-old she-goat, a three-year-old ram
     a turtle-dove and a fledgling
10   He took all these, slit them down the middle
     and gave each section opposite its companion
     The birds he did not slit
11   The birds of prey came down upon the corpses
     Abram shooed them away
12   The sun was going down
     a swoon fell upon Abram
     Here! fright, great darkness, fell upon him

13   He said to Abram, Know! you shall know
     that your seed will sojourn in a land not theirs
     They will serve them and be afflicted by them
     for four hundred years
14   But that nation they serve I will judge
     Afterwards they shall go out with great gain
15   And you, you shall come to your fathers in peace
     You shall be entombed at a good hoar age
16   In the fourth age they shall return here
     for the Amorites' wrong-doing will not be complete
     until then

17   The sun went down
     there was thick darkness
     and here! a smoking oven and a torch of fire
     which passed between the pieces
18   On that day YHWH cut a pact with Abram, saying,
     To your seed I give this land
     from the river of Egypt to the great river
     the river Euphrates

19 the Kenites, the Kenizzites, the Kadmonim
20 the Hittites, the Perizzites, the Rephaim
21 the Amorites, the Canaanites, the Girgashites, the Jebusites

CHAPTER 16

1   Sarai, Abram's woman, had not bred for him
    She had an Egyptian maid Her name was Hagar
2   Sarai said to Abram
    Look! YHWH has obstructed me from child-birth
    Go in to my maid
    Perhaps I shall build myself a son through her
    Abram heard Sarai's voice
3   Abram's woman Sarai took her maid Hagar the Egyptian
    ten years after Abram had settled in the land of Canaan
    She gave her to her man Abram, as his woman
4   He went in to Hagar and she conceived
    and saw that she had conceived
    Her mistress was less in her eyes!
5   Sarai said to Abram
    The outrage done to me is on you!
    I, I gave my maid into your bosom
    But she sees that she has conceived
    and I am less in her eyes
    Let YHWH judge between me and you!
6   Abram said to Sarai
    Here, your maid is in your hand
    Do to her what is good in your eyes
    Sarai so afflicted her that she fled from her

7   YHWH's messenger found her
    by the pool of water in the wilderness
    by the pool on the road to Shur
8   He said, Hagar, maid of Sarai!

Where have you come from? Where are you going to?
She said, I am fleeing from my mistress Sarai

9   YHWH's messenger said to her
Return to your mistress
be afflicted under her hands

10   YHWH's messenger said to her
Increase! I will increase your seed
it shall be too abundant to be counted

11   YHWH's messenger said to her
Here, you have conceived and shall breed a son
You shall call his name God Hears (Ishmael)
for YHWH has heard your affliction

12   He shall be a wild ass of a man
his hand against all, the hand of all against him
Facing all his brothers he shall dwell

13   She called the name of YHWH who had spoken to her
You, God of seeing (El Roi)!
for she said, Have I not seen also after he saw me?

14   So they called the well
Well of the Living One Who Sees Me (Beer-lahai-roi)
Here, it is between Kadesh and Bered

15   Hagar bred a son for Abram
Abram called the name of his son
who Hagar bred, Ishmael

16   Abram was eighty-six years old
when Hagar bred Ishmael for Abram

13 Last line: Hebrew obscure.

CHAPTER 17

1 Abram was ninety years old
   when YHWH was seen by Abram and said to him
   I, El Shaddai!
   Walk before me! Be whole!
2 I give my pact between me and you
   I will increase you exceedingly

3 Abram fell upon his face
   Elohim spoke with him, saying
4 I! Here is my pact with you
   you shall be the father of a tumult of nations
5 No longer shall your name be called Abram
   your name shall be Father of a Multitude (Abraham)
   for I give you as the father of a tumult of nations
6 I will make you exceedingly fruitful
   I will give nations of you
   Kings shall go out from you
7 I set up my pact between me and you
   and your seed after you
   through the ages as an everlasting pact
   to be Elohim to you
   and to your seed after you
8 I will give you and your seed after you
   the land of your sojourning
   all the land of Canaan as everlasting property
   I will be Elohim to them

1 El Shaddai. See Translator's Postscript. Others: God Almighty.

9 Elohim said to Abraham
  And you, you shall keep my pact
  you and your seed after you through the ages
10 This is my pact that you shall keep
  between me and you
  and your seed after you
  Every male among you shall be circumcised
11 You shall circumcise the flesh of your foreskins
  It shall be a sign of the pact between me and you
12 The eight-day-old among you shall be circumcised
  every male through the ages bred in the household
  or acquired for silver from the son of a stranger
  who is not of your seed
13 Circumcised! he shall be circumcised
  bred in your household
  or acquired with your silver
  My pact shall be in your flesh
  as an everlasting pact
14 A male with a foreskin who is not circumcised
  in the flesh of his foreskin
  that soul shall be cut off from his people
  He has nullified my pact!

15 Elohim said to Abraham
  Sarai, your woman
  you shall not call her name My Princess (Sarai)
  for Princess (Sarah) is her name
16 I will bless her
  By her also I will give you a son
  I will bless her
  She shall become nations
  Kings of peoples shall be of her
17 Abraham fell upon his face and laughed

He said in his heart
Shall a child be bred for a hundred-year-old?
And if Sarah . . .
shall a ninety-year-old breed?

18 Abraham said to the Elohim
Only let Ishmael live before you!

19 Elohim said
Still, your woman Sarah shall breed a son for you
You shall call his name He Laughs (Isaac)
I will set up my pact with him as an everlasting pact
for his seed after him

20 As to Ishmael, I have heard you
Here, I will bless him
I will make him fruitful
I will increase him exceedingly
He shall breed twelve chieftains
I will give him as a great nation

21 But my pact I will set up with Isaac
who Sarah shall breed for you at the set time
in another year

22 He finished speaking with him
Elohim went up from beside Abraham

23 Abraham took his son Ishmael
all those bred in his household
all who were acquired with his silver
every male among the men of the house of Abraham
He circumcised the flesh of their foreskins
on that very day
as Elohim had spoken to him

24 Abraham was ninety years old
when he was circumcised in the flesh of his foreskin

25 His son Ishmael was thirteen years old

when he was circumcised in the flesh of his foreskin
26 On that very day
Abraham was circumcised and his son Ishmael
27 All the men of his household
bred in the household
or acquired for silver from the son of a stranger
were circumcised with him

CHAPTER 18

1   YHWH was seen by him by the Oaks of Mamre
He was sitting at the entrance of the tent
in the heat of the day
2   He lifted up his eyes and saw
Here! three men were standing beside him
He saw
and ran to greet them from the entrance of the tent
He prostrated himself on the earth
3   He said, My lords
if I have found favour in your eyes
please do not pass by your servant
4   Let a little water be taken and bathe your feet
Lean down under the tree
5   I will take a crumb of bread
You shall sustain your hearts
Afterwards you shall pass on . . .
now that you have passed near your servant
They said, Do as you have spoken

6   Abraham hurried to the tent to Sarah
He said, Hurry! Three seahs of semolina flour!
Knead and make bread-cakes
7   To the herd Abraham ran
He took a calf, tender and good

---

3 or "My Lord"
6 Three seahs: A seah is a dry measure of 13 litres.

and gave it to the boy
who hurried to make it ready

8   He took curds, milk, the calf he had made ready
and gave these before them
He stood near them under the tree
They ate

9   They said to him
Where is your woman Sarah?
He said, Here in the tent

10   He said, Return! I will return to you at lifetide
and there shall be a son for your woman Sarah!
Sarah heard at the entrance of the tent
which was behind him

11   Abraham and Sarah were old, advanced in days
The way of women had stopped for Sarah!

12   Sarah laughed in her inwards, saying
Worn as I am, shall pleasure be for me?
And my lord is old!

13   YHWH said to Abraham
Why this? Sarah is laughing, saying
So shall I truly breed, old as I am?

14   Is anything marvellous for YHWH?
At the set time I will return to you
at lifetide and for Sarah a son!

15   Sarah dissembled, saying
I did not laugh! for she was afraid
But he said, Yes, you did laugh!

16   The men rose from there
They looked down upon the face of Sodom
Abraham went with them to send them off

17   YHWH said
I, shall I cover up from Abraham what I do?

18   Become! Abraham shall become
      a nation, great and strong
      They shall be blessed through him
      all the nations of the earth
19   For I have acknowledged him
      so that he shall command
      his sons and his house after him
      They shall keep the road of YHWH
      by doing what is just and right
      so that YHWH shall bring upon Abraham
      what he spoke of concerning him

20   YHWH said
      The outcry of Sodom and Gomorrah
      how it has increased! Their sin, how heavy!
21   Let me go down and see
      If according to the outcry that has come to me
      they have done . . . Havoc!
      If not . . . I will know

22   The men faced about from there and went towards Sodom
      but Abraham still stood before YHWH
23   Abraham drew closer and said
      So will you sweep away the just with the criminals?
24   Perhaps there exist fifty just amidst the town?
      So will you sweep them away?
      Will you not bear the place
      for the fifty just who are within it?
25   Profanation! You do such a thing!
      Put to death the just with the criminals!
      Shall it be for the just as for the criminals?
      Profanation!
      Will not the judge of all the earth do justice?

26   YHWH said
If I find in Sodom fifty just amidst the town
I will bear all the place because of them

27   Abraham answered and said
Look, I have undertaken to speak to my Lord
I, soil and ashes!

28   Perhaps of the fifty just, five are wanting!
Will you destroy all the town for the five?
He said I will not destroy it, if I find forty-five there

29   He spoke to him again once more and said
Perhaps forty will be found there?
He said, I will not do it because of the forty

30   He said, Let it not inflame my Lord
I will speak
Perhaps thirty will be found there?
He said, I will not do it, if I find thirty there

31   He said, Look, I have undertaken to speak to my Lord
Perhaps twenty will be found there?
He said, I will not destroy it because of the twenty

32   He said, Let it not inflame my Lord
I will speak this time only
Perhaps ten will be found there?
He said, I will not destroy it because of the ten

33   YHWH went away when he had finished
speaking to Abraham
Abraham returned to his place

CHAPTER 19

1   The two messengers came to Sodom in the evening
Lot was sitting at the gate of Sodom
Lot saw and rose to greet them
He prostrated himself, face to the earth

2   He said
Look, my lords!
Please turn aside to your servant's house
spend the night, bathe your feet
and you shall go early on your road
They said, No!
for we will spend the night in the square

3   He pressed them much
They turned aside to him and came into his house
He made a feast for them and baked unleavened bread
They ate

4   Before they lay down
the men of the town, the men of Sodom
surrounded the house
from young to old, all the people from every end

5   They called to Lot and said to him
Where are the men who came to you this night?
Bring them out to us and we will know them

6   Lot went out to them at the entrance
He shut the door behind him

7   He said, Please, my brothers, do no harm

8   Look, I have two daughters who have known no man
Let me bring them out to you

Do to them what is good in your eyes
Only do nothing to these men
now that they have come to the shade of my beam

9   They said, Draw back!
They said, This one came to sojourn
Judge! shall he judge?
Now we will do more harm to you than to them
They pressed the man Lot much
They drew closer to break the door

10   But the men put out their hand
and brought Lot in to them into the house
They shut the door

11   And the men at the entrance of the house
they struck with dazzlement from young to old
so that they wearied of finding the entrance

12   The men said to Lot
Who else have you here?
A son-in-law, your sons, your daughters
whoever you have in the town
bring them out of the place

13   For we will destroy this place
yes, great is their outcry before YHWH
and YHWH has sent us to destroy it

14   Lot went out
and spoke to his sons-in-law, takers of his daughters
He said, Rise, go out of this place
for YHWH will destroy the town
But he was as one jesting in his sons-in-law's eyes

15   As the dawn went up
the messengers hastened Lot, saying
Rise, take your woman

and your two daughters who are found here
or you will be swept away
in the punishment of the town

16 He lingered
The men gripped his hand, his woman's hand
the hand of his two daughters
for YHWH had pity on him
They brought him out
and set him to rest outside the town

17 When they had brought them outside, he said
Escape for your soul! Do not look behind you!
Do not stop in all the circuit!
Escape to the mountain or you will be swept away!

18 Lot said to them
No, my lord!

19 Look, your servant has found favour in your eyes
Great is the kindness you have done me
to keep my soul alive
but I am not able to escape to the mountain
or harm will cling to me and I shall die!

20 Look, this town is near to flee to
It is little
Let me escape there
—is it not little?—and my soul shall live!

21 He said to him
I have lifted your face in this thing also
I will not overthrow the town you speak of

22 Hurry! Escape there
for I am not able to do anything till you come there
So they called the name of the town Little (Zoar)

23 The sun went out upon the earth and Lot came to Zoar
24 Then YHWH rained upon Sodom and Gomorrah

brimstone and fire from YHWH from the skies
25   He overthrew those towns and all the circuit
all who were settled in the towns
whatever had sprouted on the ground
26   His woman looked behind him
She became a post of salt

27   Abraham went early in the morning
to the place where he had stood facing YHWH
28   He looked down upon the face of Sodom and Gomorrah
upon all the face of the land of the circuit
He saw, Here! the fumes of the land went up
like the fumes of the furnace
29   When Elohim destroyed the towns of the circuit
Elohim remembered Abraham
He sent Lot away from amidst the overthrow
when he overthrew the towns where Lot had settled

30   Lot went up from Zoar
and settled in the mountain
his two daughters with him
for he was afraid to settle in Zoar
He settled in a cave, he and his two daughters
31   The first-born said to the younger
Our father is old
and there is no man to come upon us
as was the way of all the earth
32   Come, we will give our father wine to drink
We will lie with him
and preserve seed alive through our father!

33   They gave their father wine to drink that night

The first-born came in and lay with her father
He did not know of her lying down or of her rising

34 On the morrow the first-born said to the younger
Here, yesterday night I lay with my father
We will give him wine to drink this night also
Come in, lie with him
We will preserve seed alive through our father

35 That night also they gave their father wine to drink
The younger one rose and lay with him
He did not know of her lying down or of her rising

36 Lot's two daughters conceived by their father
37 The first-born bred a son
She called his name From Father (Moab)
He is the father of the Moabites of today

38 The younger one also bred a son
She called his name Son of My People (Ben Ami)
He is the father of the Ammonites of today

CHAPTER 20

1   Abraham set out from there for the land of the Negeb
he settled between Kadesh and Shur
He sojourned in Gerar

2   Abraham said of his woman Sarah
She is my sister!
Abimelech king of Gerar sent and took Sarah

3   But Elohim came to Abimelech in a dream at night
and said to him, Here! you shall die
because of the woman you have taken
She is married to a husband!

4   Abimelech had not been near her
He said, My Lord
will you kill a nation, even though it is just?

5   Did he not say to me, She is my sister?
She also she said, He is my brother!
With whole heart and blameless palms I did this!

6   Elohim said to him in a dream
I also, I know that with whole heart you did this
I also, I held you back from sinning against me
and so did not give you to touch her

7   Now return the man's woman
Yes, he is an inspired one
He will pray for you and you shall live
But if you do not return her
know that die! you shall die, you and all yours

8   Abimelech up early in the morning
called all his servants

and spoke all these things in their ears
The men were very afraid

9   Then Abimelech called Abraham and said to him
What have you done to us?
In what have I sinned against you
that you have brought on me and on my kingdom
so great a sin?
Deeds that are not done you have done to me

10   Abimelech said to Abraham
What did you see that you did this thing?

11   Abraham said, Yes, I said
not the least fear of Elohim in this place!
They will kill me because of my woman

12   Also truly she is my sister, my father's daughter
but not my mother's daughter
She became my woman

13   When Elohim made me stray from my father's house
I said to her
Let this be your kindness you do me
In every place we come to, say of me
He is my brother!

14   Abimelech took flocks and herds, servants and maids
and gave them to Abraham
He returned his woman Sarah to him

15   Abimelech said, Here is my land before you
settle wherever it is good in your eyes

16   To Sarah he said, Here, I have given
a thousand silver pieces to your brother

13 Elohim is here construed with a plural verb in the Hebrew text, cf. 31, 53 &
35, 7.

Here, let it be for you a covering for the eyes
of all who are with you
You have been approved before all

17   Abraham prayed the Elohim
Elohim healed Abimelech
his woman and his maids: they bred
18   For obstructed! YHWH had obstructed every womb
in Abimelech's household
on account of Abraham's woman Sarah

16 Second half of verse: meaning of Hebrew obscure.

CHAPTER 21

1   YHWH took charge of Sarah as he had said
       YHWH did to Sarah what he had spoken of
2   Sarah conceived and bred a son for Abraham
       in his old age
       at the set time that Elohim had spoken to him of
3   Abraham called the name of his son bred for him
       whom Sarah bred for him, He Laughs (Isaac)
4   Abraham circumcised his son Isaac
       when he was eight days old
       as Elohim had commanded him
5   Abraham was a hundred years old
       when his son Isaac was bred for him
6   Sarah said, Elohim has made laughter for me!
       All that hear will laugh for me!
7   She said, Who would have declared to Abraham
       Sarah suckling sons!
       Yes, I have bred a son for his old age!
8   The child grew and was weaned
       Abraham made a great feast
       on the day that Isaac was weaned

9   Sarah saw the son of Hagar the Egyptian
       whom she had bred for Abraham, laughing . . .
10   She said to Abraham
       Cast out this slave-woman and her son
       for the son of this slave-woman shall not inherit
       with my son, with Isaac!
11   The thing was very bad in Abraham's eyes

      because of his son

12 Elohim said to Abraham
      Do not let this be bad in your eyes
      because of the boy and because of your slave-woman
      Whatever Sarah says to you
      hear her voice
      for through Isaac seed shall be called after you

13 But the son of the slave-woman also
      I will set up as a nation
      for he is your seed

14 Abraham up early in the morning
      took bread and a bottle of water
      He gave them to Hagar
      setting them upon her shoulder
      then the child
      He sent her away
      She went and strayed in the wilderness of Beer-sheba

15 The water from the bottle was finished
      She threw the child under one of the shrubs

16 She went and sat down opposite, a bowshot away
      for she said, I will not see the child die!
      She sat opposite, lifted up her voice and wept

17 Elohim heard the boy's voice
      Elohim's messenger called to Hagar from the skies
      and said to her, What is the matter, Hagar?
      Do not be afraid
      for Elohim has heard the boy's voice, there where he is

18 Rise, lift the boy, grip him with your hand
      for I will set him up as a great nation

19 Elohim opened her eyes: she saw a well of water

She went, filled the bottle with water
and let the boy drink

20   Elohim was with the boy
He grew up and settled in the wilderness
He became a master-bowman
He settled in the wilderness of Paran
21   His mother took him a woman from the land of Egypt

22   At that time Abimelech, with Pichol Chief of his troops
said to Abraham, Elohim is with you in all you do!
23   Now swear to me here by Elohim
If you play false with me
with my progeny or my posterity . . . !
As I have done kindness to you
so do to me
and to the land in which you sojourn
24   Abraham said, I swear

25   Abraham reproved Abimelech because of the well of water
that Abimelech's servants had robbed him of
26   Abimelech said, I do not know who did this thing!
You never told me
nor did I hear of it myself until today

27   Abraham took flocks and herds
he gave them to Abimelech
The two of them cut a pact
28   Abraham stood seven ewe-lambs of the flock apart
29   Abimelech said to Abraham
What are those seven ewe-lambs you have stood apart?
30   He said

You shall take these seven ewe-lambs from my hand
as my witness that I dug this well

31 So they called that place Well of Oath (Beer-sheba)
for the two of them swore there

32 They cut a pact at Beer-sheba
Abimelech rose up, with Pichol Chief of his troops
They returned to the land of the Philistines

33 He planted a tamarisk at Beer-sheba
There he called upon the name of YHWH El Olam

34 Abraham sojourned in the land of the Philistines
many days

31 Well of Oath or Well of Seven.

33 El Olam. See Translator's Postscript. Others: the Everlasting God

CHAPTER 22

1   After these things Elohim tried Abraham
    He said to him, Abraham!
    He said, Here I am

2   He said, Please take your son
    your one and only that you love, Isaac
    Go to the land of Seeing (Moriah)
    offer him up there as an offering
    on one of the mounts that I will say to you

3   Abraham up early in the morning
    bridled his ass
    He took two of his boys with him and his son Isaac
    He split the wood for the offering
    He rose and went to the place
    that the Elohim had said to him

4   On the third day
    Abraham lifted up his eyes and saw the place from afar

5   Abraham said to his boys
    Stay here with the ass
    I and the boy will go yonder
    We will prostrate ourselves and return to you

6   Abraham took the wood for the offering
    he set it upon his son Isaac
    He took in his hand the fire and the knife
    The two of them went on together

7   Isaac said to his father Abraham
    he said, My father!

He said, Here I am, my son!
He said, Here is the fire and the wood
but where is the youngling for the offering?

8   Abraham said
Elohim will see to the youngling for the offering, my son!
The two of them went on together

9   They came to the place that the Elohim had said to him
Abraham built the altar there and laid out the wood
He tied up his son Isaac
and set him upon the altar on top of the wood

10   Abraham put out his hand
and took the knife to slay his son

11   But YHWH's messenger called to him from the skies
and said to him, Abraham! Abraham!
He said, Here I am

12   He said, Do not put out your hand to the boy
do nothing to him!
Yes, now I know that you fear Elohim
you have not held back your son
your one and only, from me!

13   Abraham lifted up his eyes and saw
there was a ram behind
caught in the thicket by its horns
Abraham went and took the ram
He offered it up as an offering in place of his son

14   Abraham called the name of that place YHWH Sees
hence today's saying, On YHWH's mount is seen!

15   YHWH's messenger called to Abraham
a second time from the skies

16   He said

13 behind: Others read "one" ram.

84

By myself, I swear! Utterance of YHWH!
Because you have done this thing
and did not hold back your son, your one and only
17   yes, bless! I will bless you
increase! I will increase your seed
like the stars of the skies
like the sand on the sea's lip!
Your seed shall inherit its enemies' gate!
18   They shall bless themselves through your seed
all the nations of the earth
because you heard my voice!
19   Abraham returned to his boys
They rose and went together to Beer-sheba
Abraham settled at Beer-sheba

20   After these things Abraham was told, saying
Here, Milcah also has bred sons
for your brother Nahor
21   Uz his first-born, his brother Buz
and Kemuel the father of Aram
22   Chesed, Hazo, Pildash, Jidlaph and Bethuel
23   —Bethuel bred Rebekah—
These eight Milcah bred for Abraham's brother Nahor
24   His concubine—her name was Reumah—also bred
Tebah, Gaham, Tahash and Maacah

CHAPTER 23

1   Sarah's life was a hundred and twenty-seven years
    the years of Sarah's life
2   Sarah died at Kiriath-arba, that is Hebron
    in the land of Canaan
    Abraham came to bewail Sarah and to weep for her

3   Abraham rose from the face of his dead
    and spoke to the Sons of Heth, saying
4   I am a sojourner settled among you
    Give me entombment property among you
    and I will entomb my dead away from my face
5   The Sons of Heth answered Abraham, saying to him
6   Hear us, my lord!
    You are a Elohim's chieftain in our midst
    In the choicest of our tombs entomb your dead
    None of us will keep back his tomb from you
    for entombing your dead!
7   Abraham rose and prostrated himself
    before the People of the Land, the Sons of Heth
8   He spoke to them, saying
    If you are willing
    to entomb my dead away from my face, hear me!
    Entreat Ephron son of Zohar for me
9   he shall give me the cave of Machpelah
    that is his, at the end of his field
    For the full price he shall give it to me, in your midst
    for entombment property

10 Ephron was seated among the Sons of Heth
   Ephron the Hittite answered Abraham
   in the hearing of the Sons of Heth
   before all who came in the gate of his town, saying
11 No, my lord! Hear me!
   The field I give to you
   The cave that is in it? I give it to you
   Before the eyes of the Sons of My People
   I give it to you
   Entomb your dead!
12 Abraham prostrated himself
   before the People of the Land
13 He spoke to Ephron
   in the hearing of the People of the Land, saying
   Ah! if you will only hear me!
   I will give the silver for the field
   Take it from me and I will entomb my dead there
14 Ephron answered Abraham, saying to him
15 My lord, hear me!
   The land is four hundred shekels of silver
   What is that between me and you?
   Entomb your dead!
16 Abraham heard Ephron
   Abraham weighed out for Ephron the silver
   that he had spoken of in the hearing of the Sons of Heth
   four hundred shekels of silver at trader rate

17 Thus was established the field of Ephron
   that is in Machpelah which faces Mamre
   the field and the cave that is in it
   and all the trees in the field
   within all its surrounding border
18 as an acquisition for Abraham

before the eyes of the Sons of Heth
of all who came in the gate of his town

19 Afterwards Abraham entombed his woman Sarah
in the cave of the field of Machpelah
facing Mamre, that is Hebron
in the land of Canaan

20 Thus was established the field
and the cave that is in it for Abraham
as entombment property from the Sons of Heth

CHAPTER 24

1   Abraham was old, advanced in days
     YHWH had blessed Abraham in everything

2   Abraham said to his servant, the elder of his household
     who ruled over all he had
     Set your hand please under my thigh
3   I will make you swear by YHWH the Elohim of the skies
     and the Elohim of the earth
     that you will not take a woman for my son
     from the daughters of the Canaanites
     among whom I have settled
4   Yes, you shall go to my land and to my kin
     to take a woman for my son, for Isaac
5   The servant said to him
     Perhaps the woman will not want
     to go after me to this land
     Return, shall I make your son return
     to the land you went out from?
6   Abraham said to him
     Keep from making my son return there!
7   YHWH the Elohim of the skies
     who took me from my father's house
     and from the land of my kin
     who spoke to me
     who swore to me, saying
     To your seed I will give this land!
     he himself will send his messenger before you
     You shall take a woman for my son from there!

8   And if the woman does not want to go after you
       you shall be freed from this oath of mine
       Only do not make my son return there!

9   The servant set his hand under his lord Abraham's thigh
       and swore to him about this thing

10   The servant took ten camels from his lord's camels
       and went, all his lord's best in his hand
       he rose and went to Aram-naharaim
       to Nahor's town

11   He made the camels kneel outside the town
       by the well of water at eventide
       at the time when the water-drawers go out

12   He said, YHWH Elohim of my lord Abraham!
       Please make it happen for me today
       Do kindness to my lord Abraham!

13   Here am I standing by the pool of water
       and the daughters of the men of the town
       are going out to draw water

14   The girl to whom I say
       Please turn your pitcher and I will drink!
       and who says, Drink
       and I will also let your camels drink
       her you approve of for your servant, for Isaac
       By her I shall know
       you have done kindness to my lord

15   Before he had finished speaking
       here, Rebekah came out
       —she who was bred for Bethuel son of Milcah
       the woman of Abraham's brother Nahor—
       her pitcher on her shoulder

16   The girl was very beautiful to see
       a virgin—no man had known her

She went down to the pool
filled her pitcher and went up again

17   The servant ran towards her and said
Please let me swallow a little water from your pitcher!

18   She said, Drink, my lord
She hurried to let down her pitcher onto her hand
and let him drink

19   When she had finished letting him drink, she said
I will also draw for your camels
until they have finished drinking

20   She hurried, spilled out her pitcher in the trough
and again ran to the well to draw
She drew for all his camels

21   The man looked at her
keeping silent to know
Had YHWH made his way prosper or not?

22   When the camels had finished drinking
the man took a gold nose-ring
its weight, a half-shekel
and two bracelets for her hands
their weight, ten of gold

23   He said, Whose daughter are you? Please tell me!
Is there in your father's house
a place for us to spend the night?

24   She said to him
I am the daughter of Bethuel son of Milcah
whom she bred for Nahor

25   She said to him
Both straw and fodder with us in abundance
and a place to spend the night also

26   The man bowed down prostrate before YHWH

27   He said, Blessed is YHWH Elohim of my lord Abraham

who has not abandoned his kindness and truth to my lord
Myself on the road, YHWH has led me
to the house of my lord's brothers!

28   The girl ran and told her mother's household
according to these words

29   Rebekah had a brother His name was Laban
Laban ran to the man outside by the pool

30   When he saw the nose-ring
and the bracelets on his sister's hands
and heard his sister Rebekah's words, saying
The man spoke to me so!
he came to the man
Here he was standing by the camels by the pool

31   He said, Come, blessed of YHWH!
Why do you stand outside?
Myself, I have cleared the house
and a place for the camels

32   The man came into the house
He loosened the camels
He gave straw and fodder for the camels
and water to bathe his feet
and the feet of the men with him

33   He set food before him
but he said, I will not eat until I have spoken my speech
He said, Speak!

34   He said, I am Abraham's servant

35   YHWH has blessed my lord much
He has grown great
He has given him flocks and herds, silver and gold,
servants and maids, camels and asses

36   Sarah, my lord's woman

bred a son for my lord in her old age
and he has given him all he has

37 My lord made me swear, saying
You shall not take a woman for my son
from the daughters of the Canaanites
in whose land I have settled

38 No, you shall go to my father's house, to my clan
to take a woman for my son

39 I said to my lord
Perhaps the woman will not go after me

40 He said to me
YHWH, before whom I walk
will send his messenger with you
and make your road prosper
You shall take a woman for my son
from my clan, from my father's house

41 Only then shall you be freed from my bond
Yes, you shall come to my clan
and if they do not give her to you
you shall be free of my bond

42 I came today to the pool and I said
YHWH, Elohim of my lord Abraham
if it pleases you to prosper my road that I go on!

43 Here am I standing by the pool of water
let the maiden who comes out to draw, to whom I say
Please let me drink a little water from your pitcher

44 and who says to me
Drink and I will also draw for your camels
let her be the woman
YHWH approves of for my lord's son

45 Before I had finished speaking to my heart
here, Rebekah came out

her pitcher on her shoulder
She went down to the pool to draw
I said to her, Please let me drink!

46 She hurried, let down her pitcher from off her
and said, Drink and I will also let your camels drink
I drank and she also let the camels drink

47 I asked her, I said, Whose daughter are you?
She said, The daughter of Bethuel son of Nahor
whom Milcah bred for him
I set the ring on her nostril
and the bracelets on her hands

48 I bowed down prostrate before YHWH
and I blessed YHWH, Elohim of my lord Abraham
who had led me on the road of truth
to take the daughter of my lord's brother for his son

49 Now if you are willing to do kindness and truth to my lord
tell me
If not, tell me
Then I will face about to the right or to the left

50 Laban answered with Bethuel They said
The word has gone out from YHWH
We are not able to speak to you bad or good

51 Here is Rebekah before you
Take her and go
She shall be the woman of your lord's son
as YHWH has spoken

52 When Abraham's servant heard their words
he prostrated himself on the earth before YHWH

53 The servant brought out silver things
gold things and garments

He gave them to Rebekah
He gave bounties to her brother and to her mother

54   They ate and drank, he and the men with him
then they spent the night
They rose in the morning
and he said, Send me off to my lord!

55   Her mother and her brother said
Let the girl stay with us some days, or ten
Afterwards she shall go

56   He said to them, Do not delay me
YHWH has made my road prosper
Send me off and I will go to my lord

57   They said, We will call the girl
We will ask her mouth!

58   They called Rebekah and said to her
Will you go with this man?
She said, I will go!

59   They sent their sister Rebekah and her nurse
with Abraham's servant and his men

60   They blessed Rebekah and said to her
Our sister! you shall become thousands of myriads
Your seed shall inherit the gate of its haters

61   Rebekah rose together with her girls
They rode the camels and went after the man
The man took Rebekah and went away

62   Isaac had come . . . from Beer-lahai-roi
—he had settled in the land of the Negeb

63   Isaac went out to ponder in the field
at the turn of the evening

63 to ponder: meaning of Hebrew uncertain.

He lifted up his eyes and saw
Here, camels were coming!

64   Rebekah lifted up her eyes and saw Isaac
She fell off the camel

65   She said to the servant
Who is that man coming towards us in the field?
The servant said, It is my lord!
She took a veil and covered herself

66   The servant recounted to Isaac
all the things he had done

67   Isaac brought her into the tent of his mother Sarah
He took Rebekah, she became his woman
He loved her
Isaac was comforted after his mother

CHAPTER 25

1 Once more Abraham took a woman
  Her name was Keturah
2 She bred for him Zimran and Jokshan
  Medan and Midian, Ishbak and Shuah
3 Jokshan bred Sheba and Dedan
  The sons of Dedan
  were the Asshurim, the Letushim and the Leummim
4 The sons of Midian
  were Ephah, Epher, Hanoch, Abida and Eldaah
  All these were Keturah's sons

5 Abraham gave all he had to Isaac
6 To the sons of Abraham's concubines
  Abraham gave gifts
  and he sent them away from his son Isaac
  while he was still alive
  eastwards to the land of the East

7 These are the days of the years of Abraham's life
  which he lived, 175 years
8 Abraham passed away and died
  at a good hoar age, old and replete
  He was gathered to his people
9 His sons Isaac and Ishmael entombed him
  in the cave of Machpelah
  in the field of Ephron son of Zohar the Hittite
  which faces Mamre
10 the field that Abraham had acquired

from the Sons of Heth
There Abraham was entombed and his woman Sarah
11 After Abraham's death Elohim blessed his son Isaac
Isaac settled near Beer-lahai-roi

12 These are the breedings of Ishmael son of Abraham
whom Hagar the Egyptian, Sarah's maid
bred for Abraham
13 These are the names of Ishmael's sons
by their names, according to their breedings
Ishmael's first-born, Nebaioth
Kedar, Adbeel, Mibsam
14 Mishma, Dumah, Massa
15 Hadad, Teman, Jetur, Naphish and Kedmah
16 These are the sons of Ishmael, these their names
by their villages and their encampments
twelve chieftains for their tribes
17 And these are the years of Ishmael's life, 137 years
He passed away and died
and was gathered to his people
18 They dwelt from Havilah near Shur which faces Egypt
as far as Asshur
Facing all his brothers he fell

19 These are the breedings of Isaac son of Abraham
Abraham bred Isaac
20 Isaac was forty years old when he took Rebekah
daughter of Bethuel the Aramaean of Paddan-aram
sister of Laban the Aramaean, as his woman

21 Isaac pleaded with YHWH on behalf of his woman
for she was barren

18 Facing all his brothers . . . meaning of Hebrew uncertain.

YHWH heeded his plea
His woman Rebekah conceived

22 But the sons clashed in her inwards
and she said, If this is so, of what use am I?
She went and consulted YHWH

23 YHWH said to her
 Two nations are in your bowels
 Two folks from your belly shall divide
 Folk shall be firmer than folk
 Elder shall serve younger!

24 Her days of child-birth were fulfilled
Here, twins were in her bowels!

25 The first came out reddish
like a mantle of hair all over
They called his name Esau

26 Afterwards his brother came out
his hand grasping Esau's heel
They called his name Heeler (Jacob)
Isaac was sixty years old at their birth

27 The boys grew up
Esau became a man who knew the hunt
a man of the field
Jacob was a wholesome man staying in the tents

28 Isaac loved Esau, for game was in his mouth
Rebekah loved Jacob

29 Jacob was brewing a brew
Esau came in from the field
He was tired

30 Esau said to Jacob

22 If this is so . . . meaning of Hebrew uncertain.
25 Esau, also called Seir "Hairy" and Edom, "Red". cf. 25,30 and 32,4.

Please let me gulp of the red stuff, that red stuff
for I am tired
So they called his name Red (Edom)

31 Jacob said, Sell me your birthright today!

32 Esau said, Here I am going to die!
Of what use is a birthright to me?

33 Jacob said, Swear to me today!
He swore to him and sold his birthright to Jacob

34 Jacob gave Esau bread and a brew of lentils
He ate, drank, upped and went
Esau scorned the birthright

CHAPTER 26

1   There was hunger in the land
     aside from the first hunger that had been in Abraham's days
     Isaac went to Abimelech
     king of the Philistines, in Gerar

2   YHWH had been seen by him and had said
     Do not go down to Egypt
     Dwell in the land that I say to you

3   Sojourn in this land
     I will be with you and will bless you
     for to you and to your seed I will give all these lands
     I will uphold the oath
     that I swore to your father Abraham

4   I will increase your seed
     like the stars of the skies
     To your seed I will give all these lands
     They shall bless themselves through your seed
     all the nations of the earth

5   because Abraham heard my voice
     he kept my mandate
     my commandments, my laws and my teachings

6   Isaac stayed in Gerar

7   The men of the place asked about his woman
     He said, She is my sister
     for he was afraid to say, My woman
     "lest the men of the place kill me
     on account of Rebekah
     for she is beautiful to see"

8   When his days were prolonged there
Abimelech king of the Philistines
looked out of the window and saw
Here was Isaac laughing with his woman Rebekah!

9   Abimelech called Isaac and said
Ah! Here, she is your woman!
How could you say, She is my sister?
Isaac said to him, Because I said
I will die on account of her!

10   Abimelech said, What have you done to us!
One of the people nearly lay with your woman
You would have brought guilt upon us!

11   Abimelech commanded all the people, saying
Whoever touches this man and his woman
die! he shall die

12   Isaac sowed in that land
and found that year a hundred measures
YHWH blessed him

13   The man grew great
he went on, went on growing great
till he grew very great

14   He had a stock of sheep, a stock of oxen
and abundant servants
The Philistines were jealous of him

15   All the wells his father's servants had dug
in his father Abraham's days
the Philistines choked and filled with soil

16   Abimelech said to Isaac, Go away from us
for you have become too strong for us

17   Isaac went away from there
He camped at the watercourse of Gerar
and stayed there

18   Isaac re-dug the wells of water
       that they had dug in his father Abraham's days
       that the Philistines had choked after Abraham's death
       He called their names
       the same names his father had called them

19   Isaac's servants dug in the watercourse
       and found there a well of living water

20   The herdsmen of Gerar quarrelled
       with Isaac's herdsmen, saying
       The water is ours!
       He called the name of the well Strife (Esek)
       for they strove with him

21   They dug another well and quarrelled over it also
       He called its name Opposition (Sitnah)

22   He moved on from there and dug another well
       They did not quarrel over it
       He called its name Room (Rehobot) and said
       Yes, now YHWH has made room for us
       and we shall be fruitful in the land

23   From there he went up to Beer-sheba

24   YHWH was seen by him that night and said
       I, the Elohim of your father Abraham
       Do not be afraid, for I am with you
       I will bless you and will increase your seed
       because of my servant Abraham

25   He built an altar there
       and called upon the name of YHWH
       He spread his tent there
       and there Isaac's servants hollowed out a well

26   Abimelech went to him from Gerar
       with Ahuzzath his councillor and Pichol Chief of his troops

105

27   Isaac said to them, Why have you come to me?
You, you hate me and sent me away from you!

28   They said, See! we see that YHWH has been with you
so we say, Please let there be a bond between us
between us and you
We will cut a pact with you

29   If ever you do us harm . . . !
just as we have not touched you
just as we have done you only good
and sent you away in peace
you now blessed of YHWH!

30   He made them a feast
They ate and drank

31   Up early in the morning
they swore each to his brother
Isaac sent them off
and they went from him in peace

32   That day Isaac's servants came
and told him about the well they had dug
They said to him, We have found water!

33   He called it Oath (Shibah)
so the name of the town is Beer-sheba to this day

34   Esau was forty years old
when he took as woman Judith
daughter of Beeri the Hittite
and Basemath daughter of Elon the Hittite

35   They were bitterness of breath for Isaac and Rebekah

CHAPTER 27

1 When Isaac was old
   and his eyes were dim to see with
   he called his elder son Esau and said to him
   My son!
   He said, Here I am
2 He said, Look, I am old
   I do not know the day of my death
3 Now please lift your things
   your quiver-belt and your bow
   go out into the field and hunt game for me
4 Make me the delicacies that I love
   Bring them to me and I will eat
   so shall my soul bless you
   before I die

5 Rebekah heard when Isaac spoke to his son Esau
   Esau went to the field to hunt game to bring in
6 Rebekah spoke to her son Jacob, saying
   Here, I heard your father
   as he spoke to your brother Esau, saying
7 Bring me game and make me delicacies
   I will eat and bless you before YHWH
   before my death
8 Now, my son, hear my voice as I command you
9 Please go to the flock
   Take me two good kids from there
   I will make them into delicacies for your father
   such as he loves

10   You shall bring them to your father and he will eat
so shall he bless you before his death

11   Jacob said to his mother Rebekah
Here, my brother Esau is a hairy man
and I a smooth man

12   Perhaps my father will feel me?
In his eyes I will be a mocker
I will bring doom on myself not a blessing

13   His mother said to him
Your doom upon me, my son!
Only hear my voice
Go, take them for me

14   He went, took and brought them to his mother
His mother made delicacies such as his father loved

15   Rebekah took the garments of her elder son Esau
the attractive ones that were with her in the house
She clothed her younger son Jacob

16   With the skins of the kids she clothed his hands
and the smoothness of his neck

17   She gave the delicacies and the bread she had made
into the hand of her son Jacob

18   He came to his father and said, My father!
He said, Here I am
Which one are you, my son?

19   Jacob said to his father
I am Esau your first-born
I have done as you spoke to me
Please rise, sit down and eat of my game
so shall your soul bless me!

20   Isaac said to his son
How is it you found it so hurriedly, my son!

He said
Because YHWH your Elohim made it happen for me

21 Isaac said to Jacob, Draw close and I will feel you, my son
Are you my son Esau or not?

22 Jacob drew close to his father Isaac
He felt him and said, The voice is Jacob's voice
but the hands are Esau's hands!

23 He did not recognise him
for his hands were like his brother Esau's hands
hairy
He will bless him

24 He said, Are you my son Esau?
He said, I am

25 He said, Bring it close to me
I will eat of my son's game
so shall my soul bless you
He brought it close to him and he ate
He brought him wine and he drank

26 His father Isaac said to him
Draw close please and kiss me, my son!

27 He drew close and kissed him
He smelled the smell of his garments
He blessed him and said
    See, my son's smell
    is like the smell of a field
    that YHWH has blessed

28   The Elohim shall give you
    the dew of the skies
    and the fat of the earth
    an abundance of corn and new wine

29   Peoples shall serve you
    folks prostrate themselves before you

Be master to your brothers
They shall prostrate themselves before you
your mother's sons!
Let those who curse you be cursed
Let those who bless you be blessed

30   When Isaac had finished blessing Jacob
and when Jacob had just gone out, gone out
from before his father Isaac
his brother Esau came in from his hunt!

31   He too made delicacies
and brought them to his father
He said to his father
Let my father rise and eat of his son's game
so shall your soul bless me!

32   His father Isaac said to him
Which one are you?
He said, I am your son, your first-born, Esau!

33   Isaac trembled with an exceedingly great trembling
He said, Who was it then
that hunted game and brought it to me?
I ate it all before you came and I blessed him
So blessed he shall be!

34   When Esau heard his father's words
he cried an exceedingly great and bitter cry
He said to his father
Bless me, me too, my father!

35   He said, Your brother came with trickery
and took your blessing

36   He said, Did they not call his name Heeler (Jacob)?
He has heeled me already two times!

He took my birthright
and here now he has taken my blessing!
He said, Have you not set aside a blessing for me?

37 Isaac answered and said to Esau
Here, I have set him up as your master
I have given him all his brothers as servants
With corn and new wine I have sustained him
For you then what shall I do, my son?

38 Esau said to his father
Have you only the one blessing, my father?
Bless me, me too, my father!
Esau lifted up his voice and wept

39 His father Isaac answered and said to him
    Here, of the fat of the earth
    shall your settlement be
    of the dew of the skies above

40   By your sword you shall live
    Your brother you shall serve
    But when you grow restive
    you shall rip his yoke from your neck

41 Esau bore Jacob malice
on account of the blessing
his father had blessed him with
Esau said in his heart
The days of mourning for my father draw near
I will kill my brother Jacob

42 Rebekah was told of her elder son Esau's words
She sent and called for her younger son Jacob

39 of the fat . . . of the dew . . . Others negatively: away from the fat . . .
   from the dew . . .

She said to him, Here! your brother Esau
will find comfort in killing you

43   Now, my son, hear my voice
Rise, flee to my brother Laban in Haran

44   Stay with him some days
till your brother's heat turns away

45   till your brother's anger turns away from you
and he forgets what you have done to him
I will send and take you from there
Why, shall I be bereft of the two of you in one day?

46   Rebekah said to Isaac
I loathe my life because of the daughters of Heth
If Jacob takes a woman
from the daughters of Heth like those
from the daughters of the land
what is life to me?

CHAPTER 28

1   Isaac called for Jacob and blessed him
     He commanded him and said to him
     You shall not take a woman
     from the daughters of Canaan
2   Rise! Go to Paddan-aram
     to the house of your mother's father Bethuel
     Take yourself a woman from there
     from the daughters of your mother's brother Laban
3   El Shaddai will bless you
     he will make you fruitful and increase you
     You shall become an assembly of peoples
4   He shall give you Abraham's blessing
     to you and to your seed with you
     so that you shall inherit the land of your sojourning
     which Elohim gave to Abraham
5   Isaac sent Jacob off
     He went to Paddan-aram
     to Laban son of Bethuel the Aramaean
     the brother of Rebekah mother of Jacob and Esau

6   Esau saw that Isaac had blessed Jacob
     and had sent him to Paddan-aram
     to take himself a woman from there
     and, blessing him, had commanded him, saying
     You shall not take a woman
     from the daughters of Canaan
7   Jacob had heard his father and mother
     and had gone to Paddan-aram

8   Esau saw that the daughters of Canaan were bad
    in the eyes of his father Isaac
9   Esau went to Ishmael
    and took Mahalat daughter of Ishmael son of Abraham
    the sister of Nebayot as woman besides his women
10 Jacob went out from Beer-sheba
    He went to Haran
11 He came upon the place
    and was to spend the night there
    for the sun had gone in
    He took one of the stones of the place
    and put it at his head
    He lay down in that place
12 He dreamt
    Here, a stairway stood upon the earth
    its head touching the skies
    Here, Elohim's messengers were going up and down on it
13 And here, YHWH stood above him and said
    Myself, YHWH the Elohim of your father Abraham
    the Elohim of Isaac
    I will give to you and your seed the land you lie upon
14 Your seed shall be as the soil of the earth
    You shall expand
    seaward, eastward, northward and to the Negeb
    They shall bless themselves through you
    all the clans of the ground
    and through your seed
15 Here, I am with you!
    I will keep you wherever you go
    I will make you return to this ground
    for I will not leave you
    till I have done what I have spoken of to you

16   Jacob woke from his sleep and said
      Surely YHWH is in this place
      and I, I did not know
17   He was afraid and said, How fearful this place is!
      This is no other than the house of Elohim
      and that the gateway of the skies
18   Jacob up early in the morning
      took the stone
      that he had put at his head
      He set it up as a monument and poured oil on its head
19   He called the name of that place House of El (Bethel)
      Otherwise Luz was the name of the town at first

20   Jacob vowed a vow, saying
      If Elohim is with me
      if he keeps me on this road I go on
      and gives me bread to eat
      and garments to clothe myself
21   and I return in peace to my father's house
      YHWH shall be my Elohim
22   This stone that I have set up as a monument
      shall be the House of Elohim
      All that you give me
      tithe! I will tithe to you

CHAPTER 29

1   Jacob lifted his feet
    and went to the land of the Sons of the East
2   He saw, Here was a well in the field
    and there, three droves of sheep crouching near it
    for from that well they gave the droves to drink
    The stone on the mouth of the well was great
3   All the droves gathered there
    then they rolled the stone from the mouth of the well
    gave the flocks to drink
    and returned the stone to the mouth of the well
    in its place

4   Jacob said to them
    My brothers, where are you from?
    They said, We are from Haran
5   He said to them, Do you know Laban son of Nahor?
    They said, We know him
6   He said to them, Peace to him?
    They said, Peace—
    and here is his daughter Ewe (Rachel)
    coming with the flocks!
7   He said, Here! it is still full day
    it is not time to gather in the live-stock
    Give the flocks to drink and go on pasturing them
8   But they said, We are not able to
    until all the droves have been gathered
    then they roll the stone from the mouth of the well
    and we give the flocks to drink

9   He was still speaking with them
      when Rachel came with her father's flocks
      for she was a shepherdess

10   When Jacob saw Rachel
      daughter of Laban his mother's brother
      and the flocks of Laban his mother's brother
      Jacob drew close
      and rolled the stone from the mouth of the well
      He gave drink to the flocks of Laban his mother's brother

11   Jacob kissed Rachel, lifted up his voice and wept

12   Jacob told Rachel that he was her father's brother
      that he was Rebekah's son
      She ran and told her father

13   When Laban heard the report about Jacob his sister's son
      he ran to greet him, embraced him
      kissed him and brought him into his house
      He recounted all these things to Laban

14   Laban said to him
      Ah! you are my bone, my flesh!
      He stayed with him the days of a month

15   Laban said to Jacob
      Because you are my brother, will you serve me for nothing?
      Tell me, what shall your hire be?

16   Laban had two daughters
      The name of the elder was Leah
      The name of the younger was Rachel

17   Leah's eyes were tender
      but Rachel was fair of form and fair to see

18   Jacob loved Rachel
      He said, I will serve you seven years
      for your younger daughter Rachel

19   Laban said, Better I give her to you

than give her to another man
Stay with me

20 Jacob served seven years for Rachel
but they were like a few days in his eyes
because of his love for her

21 Jacob said to Laban, Come! my woman!
for my days have been fulfilled
and I will go in to her

22 Laban gathered all the men of the place
and made a feast

23 In the evening, he took his daughter Leah
and brought her to him and he went in to her

24 Laban had given his maid Zilpah
to his daughter Leah as a maid

25 In the morning, Here! she was Leah!
He said to Laban, What have you done to me?
Did I not serve you for Rachel?
Why have you tricked me?

26 Laban said, It is not done in our place
to give the younger before the first-born

27 Fulfil the bridal week of this one
and we will give you that one also
for the service you will serve me
another seven years

28 Jacob did so
he fulfilled the bridal week of this one
and he gave him his daughter Rachel as his woman

29 Laban had given his daughter Rachel
his maid Bilhah as her maid

30 He went in to Rachel also
He loved Rachel also

more than Leah!
He served him again another seven years

31   YHWH saw that Leah was hated
He opened her womb
And Rachel? Barren!
32   Leah conceived and bred a son
She called his name See a Son! (Reuben!)
for she said, Yes, YHWH has seen my affliction
Yes, now my man will love me!
33   She conceived again and bred a son
She said, Yes, YHWH has heard that I was hated
and he has given me this one also
She called his name Hearing (Simeon)
34   She conceived again and bred a son
She said, Now, this time my man will adhere to me
for I have bred three sons for him
So they called his name Adhesion (Levi)
35   She conceived again and bred a son
She said, This time I will laud YHWH
So she called his name Lauded (Judah)
She stopped breeding

CHAPTER 30

1   Rachel saw she had not bred for Jacob
    Rachel was jealous of her sister
    She said to Jacob
    Come! sons for me! or I shall die!

2   Jacob's anger flamed against Rachel
    He said, Am I in the place of Elohim
    who has forbidden you fruit of the bowels?

3   She said, Here is my slave-woman Bilhah
    Go in to her
    She shall breed on my knees
    and I too will build myself a son through her

4   She gave him her maid Bilhah as woman
    Jacob came in to her

5   Bilhah conceived and bred a son for Jacob

6   Rachel said, Elohim has judged for me
    Yes, he has heard my voice and given me a son
    So she called his name He Judged (Dan)

7   Rachel's maid Bilhah conceived again
    and bred a second son for Jacob

8   Rachel said
    Twistings of Elohim I have twisted with my sister
    Yes, I have prevailed!
    She called his name My Twisting (Naphtali)

9   Leah saw that she had stopped breeding
    She took her maid Zilpah
    and gave her to Jacob as woman

10   Leah's maid Zilpah bred a son for Jacob

11   Leah said, What luck!
     She called his name Luck (Gad)

12   Leah's maid Zilpah bred a second son for Jacob

13   Leah said, What success!
     Yes, daughters will deem me successful!
     She called his name Success (Asher)

14   Reuben went during the days of the wheat harvest
     and found mandrakes in the field
     He brought them to his mother Leah
     Rachel said to Leah
     Please give me of your son's mandrakes!

15   She said to her
     Is it so little for you to take my man
     that you will also take my son's mandrakes?
     Rachel said, For sure, he shall lie with you this night
     in exchange for your son's mandrakes

16   Jacob came in from the field in the evening
     Leah went out to greet him and said
     You shall come in to me
     for hired! I have hired you with my son's mandrakes
     He lay with her that night

17   Elohim heard Leah
     She conceived and bred a fifth son for Jacob

18   Leah said, Elohim has given me my hire
     for I gave my maid to my man
     She called his name Man-Hire (Issachar)

19   Leah conceived again
     and bred a sixth son for Jacob

20   Leah said, Elohim has endowed me with a good endowment
     This time my man will gratify me
     for I have bred six sons for him
     She called his name Gratified (Zebulun)

21   Afterwards she bred a daughter
      She called her name Dinah

22   Elohim remembered Rachel
      Elohim heard her and opened her womb
23   She conceived and bred a son
      She said, Elohim has removed my disgrace!
24   She called his name He Adds (Joseph), saying
      Let YHWH add another son to me!
25   When Rachel bred Joseph, Jacob said to Laban
      Send me off!
      I will go to my place, to my land
26   Give my women and my children
      for whom I have served you
      and I will go
      for you yourself know my service
      how I have served you

27   Laban said to him
      Please if I have found favour in your eyes . . .
      I have divined
      YHWH has blessed me for your sake!
28   He said, Fix me your hire and I will give it!
29   He said to him
      You yourself know how I have served you
      what has become of your live-stock under me
30   for the little you had before me
      has expanded to abundance
      YHWH has blessed you in my footsteps
      Now when shall I too do something for my household?
31   He said, What shall I give you?

24 Joseph, the name is also connected with asaph, he removed v. 23.

Jacob said, You shall give me nothing
If you will do this thing for me
I will turn back to pasture and keep your flocks

32   Let me pass among all your flocks today
putting aside from there every youngling
that is speckled or spotted
every brown youngling among the sheep
and the speckled and spotted among the goats
These shall be my hire

33   Let my justness answer for me one day tomorrow
when you come with my hire before you
Whichever is not speckled or spotted among the goats
or brown among the sheep
will be as though thieved by me!

34   Laban said
Here, only let it be according to your word!

35   But that day he put aside the he-goats
the striped and the spotted
and all the speckled and spotted she-goats
every one that had white on it
and all the brown among the sheep
He gave them into the hand of his sons

36   He set three days of road between himself and Jacob
Jacob was pasturing Laban's flocks, those left over

37   Jacob took fresh sticks of poplar, almond and plane
He streaked white streaks on them
baring the white that was on the sticks

38   He presented the sticks he had streaked
in the runnels, in the water-troughs
where the flocks came to drink
in front of the flocks
They were in heat when they came to drink

39   The flocks were in heat near the sticks
       and the flocks bred striped, speckled and spotted
40   Jacob divided off the sheep
       He made the flocks face the striped
       and all the brown of Laban's flock
       He set droves apart for himself
       and did not put them with Laban's flocks
41   Every time the sturdier flocks were in heat
       Jacob put the sticks before the eyes of the flock
       in the runnels
       to bring them into heat next to the sticks
42   When the flock was feeble, he did not put them
       The feeble were for Laban, the sturdy for Jacob
43   The man expanded exceedingly
       he had abundant flocks
       maids and servants, camels and asses

CHAPTER 31

1   He heard the words of Laban's sons, saying
    Jacob has taken all our father had
    From what our father had he has made all this weight!
2   Jacob saw Laban's face
    Here, he was not with him
    as yesterday or the day before!
3   YHWH said to Jacob
    Return to the land of your fathers, to your kin
    I will be with you!

4   Jacob sent to call Rachel and Leah
    to the field to his flocks
5   He said to them, I see from your father's face
    that he is not with me
    as yesterday or the day before
    But my father's Elohim has been with me
6   You yourselves know
    that I have served your father with all my force
7   Your father has cheated me
    He has changed my hire ten times
    But Elohim has not given him to do me harm
8   If he said, The speckled shall be your hire
    all the flock bred speckled
    If he said, The striped shall be your hire
    all the flock bred striped
9   Elohim has delivered your father's live-stock
    and given it to me

10   At the time when the flock was in heat
I lifted up my eyes and saw in a dream
Here! the tups going up on the sheep
were striped, speckled and mottled

11   The messenger of the Elohim said to me in the dream
Jacob!
I said, Here I am

12   He said, Lift up your eyes please and see
All the tups going up on the sheep
are striped, speckled and mottled
For I have seen all that Laban has done to you

13   I, the El of Bethel
where you anointed a monument and vowed a vow to me
Now, rise and go out of this land
Return to the land of your kin

14   Rachel and Leah answered, they said to him
Do we still have a share and inheritance
in our father's house?

15   Are we not thought of as strangers by him?
For he has sold us
and eaten up! eaten up our silver also

16   Yes, all the riches Elohim has delivered from our father
are ours and our sons'!
Now, do everything Elohim has said to you

17   Jacob rose
He lifted his sons and his women onto the camels

18   He drove off all his live-stock, all his gain
that he had gained, the live-stock he had acquired

13 El. See Translator's Postscript. Others: God.

that he had gained in Paddan-aram
to go to his father Isaac in the land of Canaan

19   Laban had gone to shear his flocks
and Rachel thieved her father's idols
20   Jacob duped the heart of Laban the Aramaean
by not telling him that he was about to flee
21   He himself fled with all he had
He rose, crossed the river
and set his face towards mount Gilead

22   Laban was told on the third day
that Jacob had fled
23   He took his brothers with him
and pursued him seven days of road
He caught up with him at mount Gilead
24   Elohim came to Laban the Aramaean in a dream at night
and said to him
Keep from speaking to Jacob for good or bad!

25   Laban overtook Jacob
Jacob had pitched his tents on the Mount
and Laban pitched with his brothers on mount Gilead
26   Laban said to Jacob, What have you done?
You have duped my heart
and driven my daughters like captives of the sword
27   Why did you hide to flee and dupe me and not tell me?
I would have sent you off
with gladness, with songs, with timbrel and lyre!
28   You did not allow me to kiss my sons and daughters!
Now, you have done foolishly
29   It is in the power of my hand to do you harm

but your father's Elohim said to me yesterday night
Keep from speaking to Jacob for good or bad!

30   Now, you went, went away
for you were pining, pining for your father's house!
Why did you thieve my Elohim?

31   Jacob answered and said to Laban
Yes, I was afraid
for I said "you would rob me of your daughters"

32   Whoever you find with your Elohim shall not live!
Opposite our brothers
recognise anything of yours with me and take it
Jacob did not know that Rachel had thieved them!

33   Laban came into Jacob's tent, into Leah's tent
into the tents of the two slave-women
but he did not find them
He went out of Leah's tent and came into Rachel's tent

34   Rachel had taken the idols
put them in a camel-cushion and sat upon them
Laban felt through all the tent
but he did not find them

35   She said to her father, Let not my lord's eyes flame
if I am not able to rise before you
for the way of women is upon me!
He searched but he did not find the idols

36   This inflamed Jacob and he quarrelled with Laban
Jacob answered and said to Laban, What is my fault?
What is my sin, that you blaze after me?

37   Since you have felt through all my things
what have you found of all your household things?
Put it here

in front of my brothers and your brothers
and let them decide between us two

38   I have been with you these twenty years
Your ewes and your she-goats have not miscarried
I have not eaten the rams of your flock

39   One torn by beast I never brought to you
I myself made good the loss
From my hand you looked for it
thieved by day or thieved by night

40   Was I by day, dryness ate me, frost by night
My sleep drifted from my eyes

41   These twenty years I have been in your household
I served you fourteen years for your daughters
six years for your flocks
and you changed my hire ten times!

42   If my father's Elohim, the Elohim of Abraham
and the Dread of Isaac had not been for me
yes, now you would have sent me off empty
But my affliction and the labour of my palms
Elohim has seen
and he decided yesterday night!

43   Laban answered and said to Jacob
The daughters? My daughters! The sons? My sons!
The flocks? My flocks! All you see is mine!
But for these daughters what shall I do today
or for their sons that they have bred?

44   Now come! let us cut a pact, I and you
and let there be a witness between me and you

45   Jacob took a stone and raised it up as a monument

42 Dread: meaning of Hebrew obscure.

46   Jacob said to his brothers, Glean stones
They took stones and made a mound
and ate there by the mound

47   Laban called it Mound of Witness (Yegar-sahadutha)
and Jacob called it Mound of Witness (Galeed)

48   Laban said
This mound is witness between me and you today
So they called its name Mound of Witness

49   and The Watch (Mizpah)
for he said, YHWH will keep watch between me and you
when we are concealed each from his companion

50   If you afflict my daughters
or if you take women besides my daughters . . .
though no man is with us
see, Elohim is witness between me and you

51   Laban said to Jacob
Here is this mound and here the monument
that I have cast between me and you

52   This mound is witness and the monument is witness
that I will not pass over this mound to you
that you will not pass over this mound
and this monument to me
to do harm . . .

53   The Elohim of Abraham and the Elohim of Nahor
shall judge between us, the Elohim of their father
Jacob swore by the Dread of his father Isaac

54   Jacob sacrificed a sacrifice on the Mount
He called his brothers to eat bread
They ate bread and spent the night on the Mount

47 Mound of Witness: Yegar-sahadutha in Aramaic; Galeed in Hebrew.

53 Shall judge: the verb is conjugated in the plural, cf. note 20, 13 & 35,7.

CHAPTER 32

1   Laban up early in the morning
kissed his sons and daughters and blessed them
Laban went and returned to his place

2   Jacob went on his road
Elohim's messengers encountered him

3   Jacob said when he saw them, This is Elohim's camp!
He called the name of that place
Double Camp (Mahanaim)

4   Jacob sent messengers before him to his brother Esau
in the land of Seir, in the country of Edom

5   and commanded them, saying
Say thus to my lord, to Esau
Thus says your servant Jacob
I have sojourned with Laban and delayed until now

6   Bullocks and asses
flocks, servants and maids are mine
I send to tell my lord to find favour in your eyes

7   The messengers returned to Jacob, saying
We came to your brother, to Esau
He too is going to meet you
and four hundred men are with him!

8   Jacob was very afraid and distressed
He distributed the people that were with him
the flocks, the herds and the camels
between two camps

9   He said, If Esau comes to one camp and strikes it
     the remaining camp will escape

10   Jacob said, Elohim of my father Abraham
     Elohim of my father Isaac
     YHWH who said to me, Return to your land, to your kin
     and I will be good to you!

11   small I am for all the kindnesses and all the truth
     you have done to your servant
     For with my stick I passed this Jordan
     and now I have become two camps

12   Please deliver me from the hand of my brother
     from the hand of Esau
     for I am afraid of him, lest he come and strike me
     mother and sons alike!

13   And you yourself said, Good! I will be good to you
     I will set your seed like the sand of the sea
     which cannot be counted, it is so abundant

14   He spent the night there that night
     He took from what had come to his hand
     a present for his brother Esau

15   she-goats, two hundred; he-goats, twenty
     ewes, two hundred; rams, twenty

16   milch camels with their colts, thirty
     cows, forty; bullocks, ten
     she-asses, twenty; ass-colts, ten

17   He gave them into the hand of his servants
     each drove apart
     and he said to his servants, Pass on before me
     and set a space between drove and drove

18   He commanded the first, saying
     When my brother Esau meets you

and he asks you, saying
Whose are you and where are you going?
Whose are these before you?
19   you shall say, Your servant Jacob's
This is a present sent to my lord, to Esau
and here he is also behind us . . .
20   He commanded the second so, the third so
and all those going behind the droves so, saying
According to this word you shall speak to Esau
when you find him
21   and you shall say, Also
here, your servant Jacob is behind us
For he said, I will appease his face
with the present that goes before my face
After that I will see his face!
Perhaps he will lift up my face!
22   The present passed on before him
But he spent the night that night in the camp

23   He rose that night and took his two women
his two maids and his eleven children
and passed the passage of the Jabbok
24   He took them and passed them over the watercourse
then he passed over what he had
25   Jacob was left alone
A man wrestled with him till the dawn came up
26   He saw that he had not prevailed against him
and he touched the socket of his thigh
The socket of Jacob's thigh was dislocated
as he wrestled with him
27   He said, Send me off, for the dawn is up
but he said, I will not send you off
unless you bless me!

135

28   He said to him, What is your name?
       He said, Jacob

29   Then he said
       No longer "Jacob" shall your name be said
       but El-Contender (Israel)
       for you have contended with Elohim
       and with men and have prevailed

30   Jacob asked and said, Please tell me your name
       He said, Why do you ask my name?
       He blessed him there

31   Jacob called the name of the place The Face of El (Peniel)
       "for I have seen Elohim face to face
       yet my soul has been delivered"

32   The sun shone on him as he passed Penuel
       he was limping on his thigh

33   So the Sons of Israel do not eat the sinew of the hip
       that is against the socket of the thigh, to this day
       For he touched the socket of Jacob's thigh
       at the sinew of the hip

CHAPTER 33

1   Jacob lifted up his eyes and saw
Here, Esau was coming and with him four hundred men!
He distributed the children
between Leah, Rachel and the two maids
2   He put the maids and their children first
Leah and her children behind them
then Rachel and Joseph behind them
3   He himself passed before them
and prostrated himself upon the earth seven times
until he drew close to his brother

4   Esau ran to greet him
He embraced him, fell upon his neck and kissed him
They wept
5   He lifted up his eyes and saw the women and children
He said, Who are these with you?
He said, The children
that Elohim has favoured your servant with
6   The maids drew close, they and their children
they prostrated themselves
7   Leah too drew close with her children
they prostrated themselves
Afterwards Joseph drew close with Rachel
they prostrated themselves

8   He said, What is it to you, all this camp I met?
He said, To find favour in my lord's eyes
9   Esau said, I have an abundance, my brother!

Let what is yours be yours!

10   Jacob said, Please no!
Please if I have found favour in your eyes
take my present from my hand
since I have seen your face as one sees the face of Elohim
and you have been pleased with me!

11   Please take my blessing that is brought to you
for Elohim has favoured me and I have everything
He pressed him and he took it

12   He said, Let us set out and go on
I will go opposite you

13   But he said to him
My lord knows that the children are tender
Flocks and herds giving suck are with me
If they hustle them one day, all the flocks will die

14   Please let my lord pass on before his servant
and myself I will tend slowly onwards
in step with the caravan before me
in step with the children
until I come to my lord in Seir

15   Esau said, Please let me put with you
some of the people who are with me
But he said, Why this?
Let me find favour in my lord's eyes

16   Esau turned back that day on his road to Seir

17   Jacob set out for Succoth
built himself a house
and made huts for his live-stock
So they called the name of the place Huts (Succoth)

18   Jacob came safe to the town of Shechem
which is in the land of Canaan

—on his coming from Paddan-aram
He camped before the town

19   He acquired the field plot
where he had spread his tent
from the hand of the Sons of Hamor father of Shechem
for a hundred kesitahs

20   He stood an altar there
and called it El Elohim of Israel

CHAPTER 34

1   Dinah, Leah's daughter
    whom she had bred for Jacob
    went out to see the daughters of the land
2   Shechem son of Hamor the Hivite
    chieftain of the land, saw her
    He took her, laid her and raped her
3   But his soul clung to Dinah daughter of Jacob
    He loved the girl
    and he spoke to the girl's heart
4   Shechem said to his father Hamor
    Take me this girl-child as woman

5   Jacob had heard
    that he had defiled his daughter Dinah
    but his sons were with his live-stock in the field
    Jacob kept silent until they came in
6   Hamor father of Shechem went out to Jacob
    to speak with him
7   Jacob's sons came in from the field when they heard
    The men were pained, this inflamed them much
    For he had done a foul deed in Israel
    by lying with Jacob's daughter
    This is not done!

8   Hamor spoke with them, saying
    My son Shechem—
    his soul is attached to your daughter
    please give her to him as woman

9   Intermarry with us
      You shall give us your daughters
      and take our daughters for yourselves

10   You shall settle with us
      the land shall be before you
      Settle, traverse it and acquire property in it!

11   Shechem said to her father and her brothers
      Let me find favour in your eyes
      and whatever you say to me I will give

12   However much you increase bride-price and gifts
      I will give whatever you say to me
      but give me the girl as woman

13   Jacob's sons answered Shechem and his father Hamor
      With trickery they spoke
      because he had defiled their sister Dinah

14   They said to them, We are not able to do this thing
      to give our sister to a man that has a foreskin
      for that is a disgrace for us!

15   Only thus will we consent to you
      if you become like us
      circumcising every male among you

16   Then we will give you our daughters
      and will take your daughters for ourselves
      We will settle among you and be one people

17   But if you do not hear us and be circumcised
      we will take our daughter and go

18   Their words were good in the eyes of Hamor
      and in the eyes of Shechem son of Hamor

19   The boy did not delay to do the thing
      for he desired Jacob's daughter
      He was the most honoured of his father's house

20   Hamor came with his son Shechem
       to the gate of their town
       and they spoke to the men of their town, saying
21   These men are peaceable with us
       Let them settle in the land and traverse it
       The land lies with broad hands before them
       We will take their daughters for ourselves as women
       and give them our daughters
22   But only thus will the men consent to us
       to settle among us and be one people
       every male among us shall be circumcised
       as they are circumcised
23   Their live-stock, their acquisitions, all their cattle
       will they not be for us?
       Let us consent to them and they will settle among us

24   They heard Hamor and his son Shechem
       all who went out by the gate of his town
       They were circumcised—every male
       all who went out by the gate of his town

25   On the third day, when they were ailing
       Jacob's two sons, Simeon and Levi, Dinah's brothers
       each took his sword
       They come upon the town undisturbed
       and killed every male
26   Hamor and his son Shechem
       they killed with the mouth of the sword
       They took Dinah from Shechem's house and went out
27   Then Jacob's sons came upon the victims
       and pillaged the town
       because they had defiled their sister
28   Their flocks, their herds, their asses

what was in the town and what was in the field
they took

29 All their wealth, all their small ones and their women
they captured and pillaged
and all that was in the houses

30 Jacob said to Simeon and Levi
You have brought trouble on me
and made me stink for the settler of the land
the Canaanites and the Perizzites
I am few in number
They will gather against me and strike me
I shall be wiped out, I and my house!

31 But they said
Shall he make a harlot of our sister?

CHAPTER 35

1   Elohim said to Jacob
    Rise, go up to Bethel and settle there
    Make an altar there to the El who was seen by you
    when you fled before your brother Esau
2   Jacob said to his household and all who were with him
    Put aside the Elohim of the stranger that are in your midst
    Cleanse yourselves! Change your tunics!
3   Let us rise and go up to Bethel
    I will make an altar there to the El
    who answered me on the day of my distress
    He has been with me on the road I go on
4   They gave Jacob
    all the Elohim of the stranger that were in their hand
    and the rings that were in their ears
    Jacob buried them
    under the pistachio-tree near Shechem
5   They set out and the terror of Elohim
    was upon the towns around them
    They did not pursue Jacob's sons

6   Jacob came to Luz in the land of Canaan
    —that is Bethel—
    he and all the people that were with him
7   He built an altar there
    and called the place El of Bethel

for there the Elohim had revealed themselves to him
when he was fleeing before his brother

8   Deborah, Rebekah's nurse, died
She was entombed below Bethel under the oak
They called its name Oak of Weeping (Allon-Bacuth)

9   Elohim was seen by Jacob again
when he came from Paddan-aram
He blessed him

10 Elohim said to him, Your name is Jacob
Your name shall no longer be called Jacob
For Israel shall be your name
He called his name Israel

11 Elohim said to him, Myself, El Shaddai!
Be fruitful, increase!
A nation, an assembly of nations shall come from you
Kings shall go out from your loins

12 The land I gave to Abraham and to Isaac
I give to you
and to your seed after you I will give the land

13 Elohim went up above him
at the place where he had spoken with him

14 Jacob stood a monument in the place
where he had spoken with him, a monument of stone
He libated a libation on it and poured oil upon it

15 Jacob called the name of the place
where Elohim had spoken with him Bethel

16 They set out from Bethel
There was still a stretch of land to come to Ephrath

7 Elohim is here construed with a plural verb in the Hebrew text, cf. 20, 13 &
31, 53.

Rachel was in child-birth
and her child-birth was harsh

17   When her child-birth was at its harshest
the midwife said to her
Do not be afraid, for this one too is a son for you

18   As her soul went out—for she was dying—
she called his name Son of my Agony (Ben-oni)
But his father called him Son of the Right (Benjamin)

19   Rachel died
She was entombed on the road to Ephrath
—that is Bethlehem

20   Jacob stood a monument on her tomb
It is the monument of Rachel's tomb to this day

21   Israel set out and spread his tent beyond Migdal-eder

22   When Israel dwelled in that land
Reuben went and lay with his father's concubine Bilhah
And Israel heard . . .

Jacob's sons were twelve

23   The sons of Leah, Jacob's first-born Reuben
Simeon, Levi, Judah, Issachar and Zebulun

24   The sons of Rachel, Joseph and Benjamin

25   The sons of Rachel's maid Bilhah, Dan and Naphtali

26   The sons of Leah's maid Zilpah, Gad and Asher
These were Jacob's sons
who were bred for him at Paddan-aram

27   Jacob came to his father Isaac at Mamre, Kiriath-arba
—that is Hebron—
where Abraham and Isaac had sojourned

28   The days of Isaac were 180 years

29 Isaac passed away and died
He was gathered to his people
old and replete with days
His sons Esau and Jacob entombed him

CHAPTER 36

1   These are the breedings of Esau—that is Edom

2   Esau took his women from the daughters of Canaan
     Adah daughter of Elon the Hittite
     Oholibamah daughter of Anah
     daughter of Zibeon the Hivite
3   and Basemath daughter of Ishmael
     sister of Nebaioth
4   Adah bred Eliphaz for Esau
     Basemath bred Reuel
5   Oholibamah bred Jeush, Jalam and Korah
     These are Esau's sons
     who were bred for him in the land of Canaan

6   Esau took his women, his sons, his daughters
     all the souls of his household
     all his live-stock, all his cattle
     and all his acquisitions
     that he had gained in the land of Canaan
     He went to a land away from his brother Jacob
7   for their gain was too abundant for them to settle together
     The land of their sojourning was not able to bear them
     because of their live-stock
8   Esau settled at mount Seir
     Esau—that is Edom

9   These are the breedings of Esau the father of Edom
     at mount Seir

10   These are the names of Esau's sons
     Eliphaz son of Esau's woman Adah
     Reuel son of Esau's woman Basemath
11   The sons of Eliphaz were Teman, Omar
     Zepho, Gatam and Kenaz
12   Timna was a concubine of Eliphaz son of Esau
     she bred Amalek for Eliphaz
     These are the sons of Esau's woman Adah
13   And these are the sons of Reuel
     Nahath, Zerah, Shammah and Mizzah
     These were the sons of Esau's woman Basemath
14   And these were the sons of Esau's woman Oholibamah
     daughter of Anah daughter of Zibeon
     She bred for Esau
     Jeush, Jalam and Korah

15   These are the chiefs of the Sons of Esau
     sons of Eliphaz, Esau's first-born
     chief Teman, chief Omar, chief Zepho, chief Kenaz
16   chief Korah, chief Gatam and chief Amalek
     These are the chiefs of Eliphaz in the land of Edom
     These are the sons of Adah

17   These are the sons of Reuel son of Esau
     chief Nahath, chief Zerah
     chief Shammah, chief Mizzah
     These are the chiefs of Reuel in the land of Edom
     These are the sons of Esau's woman Basemath

18   These are the sons of Esau's woman Oholibamah
     chief Jeush, chief Jalam, chief Korah
     These are the chiefs of Esau's woman Oholibamah
     daughter of Anah

19 These are the Sons of Esau and these their chiefs
   —that is Edom

20 These are the sons of Seir the Horite
   who were settled in the land
   Lotan, Shobal, Zibeon, Anah
21 Dishon, Ezer and Dishan
   These are the chiefs of the Horites
   the sons of Seir in the land of Edom
22 The sons of Lotan were Hori and Hemam
   The sister of Lotan was Timna
23 These are the sons of Shobal
   Alvan, Manahath, Ebal, Shepho and Onam
24 These are the sons of Zibeon
   Aiah and Anah
   —he is the Anah
   who found the hot springs in the wilderness
   when he was pasturing the asses of his father Zibeon
25 These are the sons of Anah
   Dishon and Oholibamah daughter of Anah
26 These are the sons of Dishon
   Hemdan, Eshban, Ithran and Cheran
27 These are the sons of Ezer
   Bilhan, Zaavan and Akan
28 These are the sons of Dishan
   Uz and Aran

29 These are the chiefs of the Horites
   chief Lotan, chief Shobal, chief Zibeon, chief Anah
30 chief Dishon, chief Ezer, chief Dishan

24 hot springs, with tradition. Meaning of Hebrew uncertain.
26 Dishon, corrected. Hebrew: Dishan.

These are the chiefs of the Horites
as to their chiefs, in the land of Seir

31   These are the kings who kinged in the land of Edom
      before a king of the Sons of Israel was king
32   Was king of Edom Bela son of Beor
      The name of his town was Dinhabah
33   Bela died Was king in his place
      Jobab son of Zerah from Bozra
34   Jobab died Was king in his place
      Husham from the land of the Temanites
35   Husham died Was king in his place
      Hadad son of Bedad
      the striker of Midian in the Field of Moab
      The name of his town was Avith
36   Hadad died Was king in his place
      Samlah of Masrekah
37   Samlah died Was king in his place
      Shaul from Rehoboth-han-nahar
38   Shaul died Was king in his place
      Baal-hanan son of Achbor
39   Baal-hanan son of Achbor died
      Was king in his place Hadar
      The name of his town was Pau
      His woman's name was Mehetabel
      daughter of Matred daughter of Mezahab

40   These are the names of the chiefs of Esau
      as to their clans, as to their places, by their names
      chief Timna, chief Alva, chief Jetheth
41   chief Oholibamah, chief Elah, chief Pinon
42   chief Kenaz, chief Teman, chief Mibzar

43   chief Magdiel, chief Iram
      These are the chiefs of Edom as to their settlements
      in the land of their property

      That is Esau the father of Edom

CHAPTER 37

1   Jacob settled in the land of his father's sojournings
in the land of Canaan

2   These are the breedings of Jacob

    Joseph, a seventeen-year old
shepherded the flocks with his brothers
He was boy to the sons of Bilhah
and the sons of Zilpah, his father's women
Joseph brought harmful slander about them
to their father

3   Israel loved Joseph more than all his sons
for he was a son of his old age
He made him an ornamented robe

4   His brothers saw that their father loved him
more than all his brothers
They hated him
and were not able to speak to him in peace

5   Joseph dreamed a dream and told it to his brothers
They hated him still more

6   He said to them, Hear please this dream I dreamed

7   Here! we were sheafing sheaves in the field
Here! my sheaf arose and stood up

---

3 ornamented robe. Others: coat of many colours. Meaning of Hebrew
uncertain.

And here! your sheaves surrounded it
and prostrated themselves before my sheaf!

8   His brothers said to him
King! will you king it over us?
Or rule! will you rule us?
They hated him still more
because of his dreams and his words

9   He dreamed again another dream
and recounted it to his brothers
He said, Here! I dreamed a dream again
And here! the sun and the moon and eleven stars
were prostrating themselves before me!

10   He recounted it to his father and his brothers
His father rebuked him and said to him
What is this dream you have dreamed?
Come! shall we come
I, your mother and your brothers
to prostrate ourselves before you on the earth?

11   His brothers were jealous of him
but his father kept the thing in mind

12   His brothers had gone
to pasture their father's flocks at Shechem

13   Israel said to Joseph
Are not your brothers pasturing at Shechem?
Go, I will send you to them
He said, Here I am

14   He said to him, Please go!
See the welfare of your brothers
and the welfare of the flock
and return me word
He sent him off from the valley of Hebron
and he came to Shechem

15 A man found him
    here, he was straying in the field
    The man asked him, saying, What are you looking for?
16 He said, I am looking for my brothers
    Please tell me where they are pasturing
17 The man said, They have set out from here
    for I heard them saying, Let us go to Dotan!
    Joseph went after his brothers
    and found them at Dotan
18 They saw him from afar
    Before he drew near them
    they conspired against him to put him to death
19 They said each to his brother
    Here comes this master of dreams!
20 Now let us go and kill him
    We will throw him in one of the pits
    We will say, A harmful beast has eaten him!
    We shall see what comes of his dreams!

21 Reuben heard and delivered him from their hand
    He said, Let us not strike at his soul!
22 Reuben said to them, Do not shed blood!
    Throw him into this pit that is in the wilderness
    but do not put a hand against him!
    so as to deliver him from their hand
    to return him to his father
23 When Joseph came to his brothers
    they stripped Joseph of his robe
    the ornamented robe that was on him
24 They took him and threw him into the pit
    The pit was empty, no water in it

25 They sat down to eat bread
    They lifted up their eyes and saw

Here! a caravan of Ishmaelites
was coming from Gilead
their camels bearing gum, balm and ladanum
that they were going to bring down to Egypt

26   Judah said to his brothers
What profit if we kill our brother
and cover up his blood?

27   Let us go and sell him to the Ishmaelites
but let not our hand be upon him
for he is our brother, our flesh!
His brothers heard him

28   Some men passed by, Midianites, traders
They dragged up Joseph from the pit
and sold Joseph to the Ishmaelites
for twenty silver-pieces
They brought Joseph to Egypt

29   Reuben returned to the pit
Here! Joseph was not in the pit!
He rent his garments

30   and returned to his brothers and said
The child is no more!
And I, where am I to go?

31   They took Joseph's robe, slew a buck of the goats
and dipped the robe in the blood

32   They sent the ornamented robe
and had it brought to their father
They said, We have found this
Please recognise whether it is your son's robe or not

33   He recognised it and said, My son's robe!
A harmful beast has eaten him!
Torn! Joseph, torn!

34   Jacob rent his tunics, set sackcloth on his hips
      and mourned his son many days
35   All his sons and all his daughters rose up
      to comfort him
      but he refused to be comforted
      He said, No!
      I will go down mourning to my son in Sheol
      His father wept for him

36   The Midianites had sold him in Egypt
      to Potiphar, Pharaoh's eunuch, the chief slaughterer

36 Midianites. Hebrew: Medanites.

CHAPTER 38

1   At that time Judah went down from his brothers
     and turned aside to a man, an Adullamite
     His name was Hirah
2   There Judah saw the daughter of a Canaanite man
     His name was Shua
     He took her and came in to her
3   She conceived and bred a son
     She called his name Er
4   She conceived again and bred a son
     She called his name Onan
5   Once again she bred a son
     She called his name Shelah
     He was in Chezib when she bred him

6   Judah took a woman for Er, his first-born
     Her name was Tamar
7   Er, Judah's first-born, was bad in the eyes of YHWH
     YHWH put him to death
8   Judah said to Onan, Come in to your brother's woman
     Be her levir and raise seed for your brother
9   Onan knew that the seed would not be his
     When he came in to his brother's woman
     he destroyed it on the earth
     so as not to give seed for his brother
10   What he did was bad in the eyes of YHWH
     He put him to death also
11   Judah said to his daughter-in-law Tamar
     Stay a widow in your father's house

until my son Shelah grows up
For he said "lest he die, he too, like his brothers!"
Tamar went and stayed in her father's house

12 Many days went by
Shua's daughter, Judah's woman, died
When Judah was comforted
he went up to the shearers of his flock
he and his companion Hirah the Adullamite, to Timnah
13 Tamar was told, saying
Here, your father-in-law is going up to Timnah
to shear his flock
14 She put aside her widow's garments from her
covered herself with a veil, wrapped herself
and sat at the entrance to Einaim
which is on the road to Timnah
For she saw that Shelah had grown up
but she had not been given to him as woman
15 Judah saw her and thought she was a harlot
for she had covered her face
16 He turned aside to her on the road
and said, Come please! Let me come in to you!
for he did not know that she was his daughter-in-law
She said, What will you give me for coming in to me?
17 He said, I myself will send you a kid from the flock
She said, If you give me a pledge until you send it
18 He said, What pledge shall I give you?
She said, Your seal and your cord
and your staff that is in your hand
He gave them to her
came in to her and she conceived by him
19 She rose, went, put aside her veil from her
and clothed herself in her widow's garments

20   Judah sent the kid
       by the hand of his companion the Adullamite
       to take back the pledge from the woman's hand
       but he did not find her
21   He asked the men of her place, saying
       Where is the cult prostitute
       the one at Einaim on the road?
       They said, There has been no cult prostitute here
22   He returned to Judah and said
       I have not found her!
       Also the men of the place said
       There has been no cult prostitute here!
23   Judah said, Let her take them for herself
       lest we be scorned
       Here, I did send the kid but you, you did not find her!

24   About three months after
       Judah was told, saying
       Your daughter-in-law Tamar has harloted
       Also here, she has even conceived from harlotry
       Judah said, Bring her out and let her be burned
25   As they were bringing her out
       she sent to her father-in-law, saying
       I have conceived by the man these belong to
       She said, Please recognise who these belong to
       the seal, the cords and the staff!
26   Judah recognised them
       He said, She is more just than I
       yes, since I did not give her to my son Shelah!
       He knew her again no more

27   At the time of her child-birth
       Here, twins were in her bowels!

28   During her child-birth one put out a hand
     The midwife took and bound scarlet on his hand
     saying, This one came out first
29   But when he took back his hand
     here, out came his brother!
     She said, What a breach you have breached for yourself!
     They called his name Breach (Perez)
30   Afterwards his brother came out
     with the scarlet on his hand
     They called his name He Shines (Zerah)

CHAPTER 39

1   Joseph was brought down to Egypt
     Potiphar, Pharaoh's eunuch, acquired him
     the chief slaughterer, an Egyptian man
     from the hand of the Ishmaelites
     who had brought him down there
2   But YHWH was with Joseph
     He became a prosperous man
     and was in the household of his Egyptian lord
3   His lord saw that YHWH was with him
     Whatever he did YHWH made prosper in his hand
4   Joseph found favour in his eyes
     and attended upon him
     Then he put him in charge of his household
     All that belonged to him he gave into his hand
5   From when he had put him in charge of his household
     and of all that belonged to him
     YHWH blessed the Egyptian's house for Joseph's sake
     YHWH's blessing was upon all he had
     in the house and in the field
6   He left all he had in Joseph's hand
     With him around, he knew of nothing
     except for the bread he ate
     Joseph was fair of form and fair to see

7   After these things
     his lord's woman lifted her eyes to Joseph
     and said, Lie with me!
8   He refused and said to his lord's woman

Here, with me around, my lord does not know
what is in the house
All that belongs to him he has given into my hand

9 He is no greater in this house than I
He has held nothing back from me
except yourself, since you are his woman
How should I do this great harm?
Shall I sin against Elohim?

10 She spoke to Joseph day after day
but he did not hear her
to lie beside her, to be with her

11 On this day
he came into the house to do his work
Not a man of the men of the house
was there in the house

12 She took hold of him by his garment, saying
Lie with me!
But he left his garment in her hand
and fled and went outside

13 When she saw he had left his garment in her hand
and fled outside

14 she called the men of her household and said to them
See! he has brought us a Hebrew man to laugh at us
He came in to me to lie with me
but I called with a great voice

15 And when he heard that I raised my voice and called
he left his garment beside me
and fled and went outside

16 She rested his garment beside her
until his lord came into his house

17 Then she spoke to him according to these words, saying

He came in to me, the Hebrew servant you brought us
to laugh at me
18   But when I raised my voice and called
he left his garment beside me and fled outside
19   When his lord heard his woman's words
that she spoke to him, saying
According to these words your servant did to me!
his anger flamed
20   Joseph's lord took him
and gave him to the round-house
the place where the king's prisoners were imprisoned
He was in the round-house
21   but YHWH was with Joseph and extended kindness to him
He gave him favour
in the eyes of the chief of the round-house
22   The chief of the round-house gave into Joseph's hand
all the prisoners that were in the round-house
Whatever they did there, it was he who had it done
23   The chief of the round-house
did not see to anything at all in his hand
because YHWH was with him
and whatever he did YHWH made prosper

CHAPTER 40

1   After these things
the butler of the king of Egypt and the baker sinned
against their lord the king of Egypt
2   Pharaoh was vexed with his two eunuchs
with the chief butler and the chief baker
3   He gave them in keeping
in the house of the chief slaughterer
in the round-house
the place where Joseph was prisoner
4   The chief slaughterer put Joseph in charge of them
and he attended upon them
They were days in keeping

5   The two of them dreamed a dream
each man his dream on one night
each man with an interpretation to his dream
the butler and the baker of the king of Egypt
who were prisoners in the round-house
6   Joseph came in to them in the morning and saw them
Here, they were enraged!
7   He asked Pharaoh's eunuchs
who were with him in keeping in his lord's house, saying
Why are your faces bad today?
8   They said to him
We have dreamed a dream
but there is no-one to interpret it!
Joseph said to them

Are not interpretations from Elohim?
Please recount them to me

9   The chief butler recounted his dream to Joseph
     He said to him
     In my dream—here! a vine was in front of me
10   On the vine were three tendrils
     As it budded, up came its blossom
     Its clusters ripened into grapes
11   Pharaoh's cup was in my hand
     I took the grapes
     squeezed them into Pharaoh's cup
     and gave the cup onto Pharaoh's palm

12   Joseph said to him
     This is its interpretation
     The three tendrils? They are three days
13   Within three days
     Pharaoh will lift up your head
     and return you to your office
     You will give Pharaoh's cup into his hand
     according to former practice, when you were his butler
14   But remember me with you, when it is well with you
     and please do me a kindness
     make Pharaoh remember me
     and get me out of this house
15   For thieved! I was thieved away
     from the land of the Hebrews
     and here too I have done nothing
     that they should have put me in the pit

16   The chief baker saw that he had interpreted for good

He said to Joseph, I too, in my dream
here! three baskets of pastry were on my head

17 In the upper basket were all foods for Pharaoh
made by baker
and the fowl were eating them
from the basket off my head

18 Joseph answered and said
This is its interpretation
The three baskets? They are three days

19 Within three days
Pharaoh will lift up your head off you
and hang you on a tree
and the fowl will eat your flesh off you

20 On the third day, Pharaoh's birthday
he made a feast for all his servants
He lifted up the head of the chief butler
and the head of the chief baker
amidst his servants

21 He returned the chief butler to his butlership
and he gave the cup onto Pharaoh's palm

22 But the chief baker he hanged
as Joseph had interpreted for them

23 The chief butler did not remember Joseph
He forgot him

16 pastry: meaning of Hebrew uncertain.

CHAPTER 41

1   At the end of two years of days Pharaoh dreamed
    Here! he was standing by the Nile
2   Here! out of the Nile went up seven cows
    fair to see and fat of flesh
    They pastured in the reed-grass
3   And here! seven other cows
    went up after them out of the Nile
    bad to see and thin of flesh
    They stood beside the cows on the lip of the Nile
4   The cows that were bad to see and thin of flesh ate up
    the seven cows that were fair to see and fat
    Pharaoh woke up!

5   He slept and dreamed a second time
    Here! seven spikes fat and good went up on one stalk
6   And here! seven thin spikes blighted by the east wind
    sprouted after them
7   The thin spikes devoured the seven fat, full spikes
    Pharaoh woke up and here, it was a dream!

8   In the morning his breath was quivering
    He sent and called all the magicians of Egypt
    and all its wise men
    Pharaoh recounted his dream to them
    but there was no-one to interpret them for Pharaoh!
9   The chief butler spoke with Pharaoh, saying
    I will call my sins to remembrance today
10 Pharaoh was vexed with his servants

and gave me in keeping
in the house of the chief slaughterer
myself and the chief baker

11   We dreamed a dream on one night, I and he
Each man with an interpretation to his dream
we dreamed

12   There was with us a Hebrew boy
a servant of the chief slaughterer
We recounted to him
and he interpreted our dreams for us
For each man according to his dream he interpreted

13   As he interpreted for us, so it was!
He returned me to my office but he hanged him!

14   Pharaoh sent and called Joseph
They made him run out of the pit
He shaved, changed his tunics and came in to Pharaoh

15   Pharaoh said to Joseph
I have dreamed a dream
but there is no-one to interpret it!
But I have heard it said of you
that you hear a dream to interpret it

16   Joseph answered Pharaoh, saying
Not I! Elohim will answer for Pharaoh's peace

17   Pharaoh spoke to Joseph
In my dream
here! I was standing on the lip of the Nile

18   Here! out of the Nile went up seven cows
fat of flesh and fair of form
They pastured in the reed-grass

19   And here! seven other cows went up after them

mean, very bad of form and lean of flesh
I have not seen their like
in all the land of Egypt for bad

20 The lean, bad cows ate up the first seven fat cows

21 They came into their inwards
but it could not be known
that they had come into their inwards
The sight of them was bad as at the beginning
And I woke up!

22 Then I saw in my dream
Here! seven spikes went up on one stalk
full and good

23 And here! seven gritty, thin spikes
blighted by the east wind, sprouted after them

24 The thin spikes devoured the seven good spikes!
I have said it to the magicians
but there is no-one to tell me!

25 Joseph said to Pharaoh
Pharaoh's dream is one
Elohim has told Pharaoh what he is about to do

26 The seven good cows are seven years
the seven good spikes are seven years
the dream is one

27 The seven lean, bad cows
going up after them are seven years
The seven empty spikes blighted by the east wind
are seven years of hunger!

28 This is the thing I spoke of to Pharaoh
The Elohim has let Pharaoh see what he is about to do

29 Here, seven years are coming
of great plenty in all the land of Egypt

30 But seven years of hunger will arise after them

All plenty will be forgotten in the land of Egypt
Hunger will consume the land

31   Plenty will be unknown in the land
because of that hunger after
for it will be very heavy

32   As to the repeating of Pharaoh's dream two times
it means that the thing is ready with the Elohim
and the Elohim is hurrying to do it

33   Now, let Pharaoh see a discerning and wise man
and put him over the land of Egypt

34   Let Pharaoh do this
let him put overseers in charge of the land
Let him take a fifth of the land of Egypt
during the seven years of plenty

35   Let them collect all food
of these good years that are coming
Let them heap up grain under Pharaoh's hand
—food for the towns—and keep it

36   The food shall be a store for the land
for the seven years of hunger
that will be in the land of Egypt
and the land shall not be cut off by the hunger

37   The word was good in Pharaoh's eyes
and in the eyes of all his servants

38   Pharaoh said to his servants
Shall we find another like this
a man with the breath of Elohim in him?

39   Pharaoh said to Joseph

34 a fifth: meaning of Hebrew uncertain.

Since Elohim has made you know all this
no-one is discerning and wise as you
40 You shall be over my house
and all my people shall kiss your mouth
Only by the throne shall I be greater than you!
41 Pharaoh said to Joseph
See! I give you over all the land of Egypt!
42 Pharaoh removed his signet-ring from his hand
and gave it onto Joseph's hand
He clothed him in garments of lawn
and set the chain of gold upon his neck
43 He had him ride in the chariot of his Second
and they called before him, Kneel!
He gave him over all the land of Egypt
44 Pharaoh said to Joseph
Myself, Pharaoh!
Without you no man shall raise his hand or foot
in all the land of Egypt!
45 Pharaoh called Joseph's name Zaphenath-paneah
He gave him Asenath daughter of Poti-phera
priest of On, as woman
Joseph went out over the land of Egypt

46 Joseph was thirty years old
when he stood before Pharaoh king of Egypt
Joseph went out from before Pharaoh
and passed through all the land of Egypt

47 The land during the seven years of plenty
produced in fistfuls

40 kiss your mouth: literal translation. Others: submit to your orders.
43 Kneel: Hebrew obscure.
45 Zaphenath-paneah, Egyptian for "God speaks, he lives".

48   He collected all the food of the seven years
     that were in the land of Egypt
     and gave the food into the towns
     The food of the field around the town
     he gave into it
49   Joseph heaped up grain like the sand of the sea
     very abundant
     till they stopped counting it
     for it was countless!

50   Two sons were bred for Joseph before the year of hunger came
     whom Asenath bred for him
     the daughter of Poti-phera priest of On
51   Joseph called the name of the first-born
     He Makes Oblivious (Manasseh)
     "for Elohim has made me oblivious of all my toil
     and all my father's house"
52   The name of the second he called Double Fruit (Ephraim)
     "for Elohim has made me fruitful
     in the land of my affliction"

53   They were finished the seven years of the plenty
     that was in the land of Egypt
54   and the seven years of hunger began to come
     as Joseph had said
     There was hunger in all lands
     but in all the land of Egypt there was bread
55   Then all the land of Egypt hungered
     and the people cried to Pharaoh for bread
     but Pharaoh said to all Egypt
     Go to Joseph! do whatever he says to you!
56   The hunger was upon all the face of the land
     and Joseph opened all that was within

and supplied Egypt
The hunger had gripped the land of Egypt
57   but from all the earth they came to Egypt
to Joseph for supplies
for the hunger had gripped all the earth

CHAPTER 42

1 Jacob saw that there were supplies in Egypt
Jacob said to his sons
Why are you looking at one another?

2 He said, Here, I have heard
that there are supplies in Egypt
Go down there, supply us from there
We shall live and not die!

3 Ten of Joseph's brothers went down
for supplies of grain from Egypt

4 But Benjamin, Joseph's brother
Jacob did not send with his brothers
for he said, Lest a disaster happen to him!

5 The sons of Israel came for supplies
among those that came
for the hunger was in the land of Canaan

6 Joseph was the vizier of the land
he it was who supplied all the people of the land
Joseph's brothers came
and prostrated themselves before him
face to the earth

7 Joseph saw his brothers and recognised them
but he was as a stranger to them
and spoke harshly with them
He said to them, Where do you come from?
They said, From the land of Canaan for supplies of food

8 Joseph recognised his brothers but they did not recognise him

9 Joseph remembered the dreams

he had dreamed about them
He said to them, You are spies!
To see the nakedness of the land you have come
10   They said to him, No, my lord!
Your servants have come for supplies of food
11   We are all of us sons of one man
We are honest
your servants have never been spies!
12   He said to them, No!
the nakedness of the land you have come to see

13   They said
Your twelve servants? We are brothers
sons of one man in the land of Canaan
Here, the youngest is with our father today
and one is no more
14   Joseph said to them
It is as I have spoken to you, saying
You are spies!
15   By this you shall be tested
As Pharaoh lives! you shall not get out of this
unless your youngest brother comes here
16   Send one of you and let him take your brother
You yourselves shall be imprisoned
Your words shall be tested
Is truth with you?
If not, as Pharaoh lives! yes, you are spies!
17   He removed them into keeping for three days

18   Joseph said to them on the third day
Do this and you shall live!
I fear the Elohim!
19   If you are honest

let one of your brothers be imprisoned
in the house of your keeping
You yourselves go, bring
supplies for the hunger of your households
20   You shall bring your youngest brother to me
Your words shall prove trustworthy
and you shall not die!
They will do so
21   But they said each to his brother
Still, we are guilty towards our brother
we saw his soul's distress, when he asked for our favour
and we did not hear him
so this distress has come upon us!
22   Reuben answered them, saying
Did I not say to you, Do not sin against the child?
But you did not hear
So here comes the reckoning for his blood!
23   They did not know that Joseph heard
for the interpreter was between them
24   He rounded from them and wept
Then he turned back to them and spoke to them
He took Simeon away from them
and imprisoned him before their eyes
25   Joseph commanded
that they fill their vessels with grain
return their silver to each man's sack
and give them provisions for the road
They did so for them
26   They lifted their supplies onto their asses
and went from there

27   As one opened his sack
to give his ass fodder at the encampment

he saw his silver
Here it was in the mouth of his bag!
28 He said to his brothers
My silver has been returned!
It is here in my bag!
Their hearts went out
Each trembled towards his brother, saying
What has Elohim done to us?

29 They came to their father Jacob in the land of Canaan
and told him all that had happened to them, saying
30 The man, the lord of the land, spoke harshly with us
He took us for spies of the land
31 We said, We are honest, we have never been spies!
32 We are twelve brothers, sons of our father
One is no more
and the youngest today is with our father
in the land of Canaan
33 The man, the lord of the land, said to us
By this I shall know that you are honest
let one of your brothers rest with me
Take for the hunger of your households and go
34 Bring your youngest brother to me
Then I shall know you are not spies
that you are honest
I will give your brother to you
and you shall traverse the land

35 When they were emptying their sacks
Here! each man's silver purse was in his sack!
They saw their silver purses, they and their father
and they were afraid
36 Their father Jacob said to them

You have bereft me!
Joseph is no more! Simeon is no more!
And will you take Benjamin?
Everything is against me!

37 Reuben spoke to his father, saying
You shall put my two sons to death
if I do not bring him back to you!
Give him into my hand
and I myself will return him to you

38 He said, My son shall not go down with you
for his brother is dead and he alone remains!
Should a disaster happen to him on the road you go on
you will bring down my hoary head in grief to Sheol!

CHAPTER 43

1 The hunger was heavy in the land
2 When they had finished eating the supplies
   that they had brought back from Egypt
   their father said to them
   Return! Supply us with a little food!
3 But Judah said to him
   The man witnessed! he witnessed against us, saying
   You shall not see my face
   unless your brother is with you!
4 If you are willing to send our brother with us
   we will go down for supplies of food for you
5 But if you are not willing to send him
   we will not go down
   for the man said to us, You shall not see my face
   unless your brother is with you!

6 Israel said, Why did you harm me
   by telling the man that you still have a brother?
7 They said, the man asked, he asked
   about us and about our kin, saying
   Is your father still alive?
   Have you a brother?
   We told him according to these words
   Did we know, know that he was to say
   Bring your brother down?

8 Judah said to his father Israel, Send the boy with me

Let us rise and go
We will live and not die, we, you and our small ones
9   I myself will be pledge for him
you shall look for him from my hand
If I do not bring him back to you
and present him before you
I shall be guilty of sin against you for all time
10   For if we had not lingered
now we would have returned two times already!

11   Their father Israel said to them
If it is so, then do this
Take of the pick of the land in your vessels
bring it down to the man as a present
a little balm, a little honey
gum, ladanum, pistachios and almonds
12   Take twice the silver in your hand
The silver returned in the mouth of your bags
you shall return in your hand
Perhaps it was a mistake
13   Take your brother! Rise, return to the man
14   El Shaddai shall give the man merciful feelings
towards you
so that he will send your other brother
and Benjamin
As to myself, if I am to be bereft, I will be bereft!

15   The men took this present
they took twice the silver in their hand
then Benjamin
They rose and went down to Egypt
and stood before Joseph

16 Joseph saw Benjamin with them
    and said to the one over his household
    Bring the men into the house
    Slaughter a slaughter animal and make ready
    for the men shall eat with me at noon
17 The man did as Joseph said
    The man brought the men into Joseph's house
18 The men were afraid
    for they had been brought into Joseph's house
    They said, On account of the silver returned in our bags
    at the beginning, we are being brought—
    to roll upon us and fall upon us
    and take us as servants with our asses!
19 They drew close to the man
    who was over Joseph's household
    and spoke to him at the entrance to the house
20 They said, I beg you, my lord!
    Came down! we came down at the beginning
    for supplies of food
21 But when we came to the encampment
    and opened our bags
    Here! each man's silver was in the mouth of his bag
    Our silver in weight!
    We have returned it in our hand
22 And other silver we have brought down in our hand
    for supplies of food
    We do not know who put our silver in our bags
23 He said, Peace to you!
    Do not be afraid!
    Your Elohim, the Elohim of your father
    has given you treasure in your bags

Your silver came to me
He brought Simeon out to them

24 The man brought the men into Joseph's house
He gave water and they bathed their feet
He gave fodder for their asses
25 They made the present ready for Joseph's coming at noon
for they had heard
that they were to eat bread there
26 Joseph came into the house
They brought him the present
that was in their hand into the house
and prostrated themselves before him on the earth
27 He asked after their peace
and said, Is he at peace, your old father
who you spoke of?
Is he still alive?
28 They said, Your servant, our father is at peace
He is still alive
They bowed down and prostrated themselves

29 He lifted up his eyes and saw his brother Benjamin
his mother's son
He said, Is this your youngest brother
who you spoke to me of?
He said, Elohim favour you, my son!
30 Joseph hurried, for his feelings warmed to his brother
and he looked to weep
He went into the chamber and wept there
31 He bathed his face, went out, controlled himself and said
Set out bread!
32 They set it out for him apart, for them apart
and for the Egyptians eating with him apart

For Egyptians are not able to eat bread with Hebrews
for that is an abhorrence to Egyptians
33 But they sat before him
the first-born according to his birthright
the youngest according to his youth!
The men looked in amazement each at his companion
34 He lifted portions for them from what was before him
Benjamin's portion increased
more than all their portions by five handfuls
They drank and became drunk with him

CHAPTER 44

1   He commanded the one over his household, saying
     Fill the men's bags with food
     as much as they are able to bear
     Set each man's silver in the mouth of his bag
2   And my goblet, the goblet of silver
     set in the mouth of the youngest one's bag
     with the silver for his supplies
     He did according to Joseph's word
     which he had spoken

3   In the morning light the men were sent off
     they and their asses
4   They went out of the town
     they have not gone far
     Joseph said to the one over his household
     Rise, pursue the men, overtake them and say to them
     Why have you paid back harm for good?
5   Is not this the one my lord drinks from?
     And divines! he divines in it!
     You have done harm by what you have done

6   He overtook them and spoke these words to them
7   They said to him
     Why does my lord speak such words?
     Profanation! Your servants do such a thing?
8   Here, the silver we found in the mouth of our bags
     we returned to you from the land of Canaan

How could we thieve from your lord's house
silver or gold?
9 Whichever of your servants it is found with shall die!
We ourselves also will become my lord's servants
10 He said, Now let it be according to your words
Whoever it is found with shall become my servant
but you shall be free of blame
11 They hurried
each man let down his bag to the earth
Each man opened his bag
12 He searched
he began with the eldest and finished with the youngest
The goblet was found in Benjamin's bag!
13 They rent their tunics
each man loaded his ass
and they returned to the town

14 Judah and his brothers came into Joseph's house
He was still there
They fell to the earth before him
15 Joseph said to them
What is this deed you have done?
Do you not know that divines! he divines
a man like me?
16 Judah said, What shall we say to my lord?
What speak, by what justify ourselves?
The Elohim has found out your servants' guilt
Here we are, my lord's servants
we and he who was found with the goblet in his hand
17 He said, Profanation! I do that!
The man who was found with the goblet in his hand
shall become my servant
But you, go up in peace to your father

18   Judah drew closer to him and said
     I beg you, my lord!
     Please let your servant speak a word in my lord's ears
     Do not let your anger flame against your servant
     for you are as Pharaoh!
19   My lord asked his servants, saying
     Do you have a father, or a brother?
20   We said to my lord
     We have an old father and a young child of old age
     His brother is dead
     He alone is left of his mother
     His father loves him
21   You said to your servants, Bring him down to me
     I will set my eyes upon him
22   We said to my lord
     The boy is not able to leave his father
     Should he leave his father, he will die!
23   You said to your servants
     If your youngest brother does not come down with you
     you shall see my face no more!
24   When we went up to your servant my father
     we told him my lord's words

25   Our father said, Return! Supply us with a little food!
26   We said, We are not able to go down
     But if our youngest brother is with us
     we will go down
     For we will not be able to see the man's face
     if our youngest brother is not with us!
27   Your servant my father said to us
     You yourselves know that my woman bred two for me
28   One went away from me and I said, Ah! torn! torn!
     I have not seen him up now

29   And you will take this one also from before my face!
     Should a disaster happen to him,
     you will bring down my hoary head in harm to Sheol

30   Now, when I come to your servant my father
     and the boy is not with us . . .
     his soul is bound to his soul!
31   When he sees that the boy is no more, he will die
     Your servants will bring down the hoary head
     of your servant our father in grief to Sheol!
32   For your servant pledged himself for the boy
     to my father, saying, If I do not bring him back to you
     I shall be guilty of sin against my father for all time
33   Now, please let your servant stay in place of the boy
     as my lord's servant
     Let the boy go up with his brothers
34   For how can I go up to my father
     if the boy is not with me?
     Let me not see the harm that would overcome my father!

CHAPTER 45

1   Joseph was not able to control himself
before all who stood about him
He called, Out! Every man away from me!
No man stood with him
when Joseph made himself known to his brothers
2   He gave his voice in weeping
Egypt heard
Pharaoh's household heard

3   Joseph said to his brothers, It is me, Joseph!
Is my father still alive?
But his brothers were not able to answer him
they were so dismayed before him

4   Joseph said to his brothers, Please draw close to me
They drew close
He said, It is me, your brother Joseph!
Me that you sold to Egypt!
5   Now, do not be pained nor let your eyes flame
because you sold me here
for it was to preserve life
that Elohim sent me on before you
6   Yes, these two years
the hunger has been in the land's inwards
and for five more years
there will be no ploughing or harvest
7   But Elohim sent me on before you

to set you as a remnant on earth
and to keep you alive in a great escape

8 Now, it was not you who sent me here but the Elohim
He set me up as father to Pharaoh
as lord of all his household
and ruler over all the land of Egypt

9 Hurry! Go up to my father and say to him
Thus says your son Joseph
Elohim has set me up as lord of all Egypt
Come down to me, do not stop!

10 You shall settle in the land of Goshen
you shall be near me
you, your sons, your sons' sons
your flocks, your herds and all that is yours

11 I will maintain you there
—for there will be five more years of hunger—
lest you be disinherited, you and your household
and all that is yours

12 Here, your eyes see, and my brother Benjamin's eyes
that it is my mouth that speaks to you

13 Tell my father of all my weight in Egypt
and of all that you have seen
Hurry! Bring my father down here

14 He fell on his brother Benjamin's neck and wept
Benjamin wept on his neck

15 He kissed all his brothers and wept upon them
After that his brothers spoke with him

16 A voice was heard in Pharaoh's house, saying
Joseph's brothers have come!
It was good in Pharaoh's eyes and in the eyes of his servants

17 Pharaoh said to Joseph, Say to your brothers

Do this, harness your animals
go, come back to the land of Canaan
18 take your father and your households and come to me!
I will give you the best of the land of Egypt
you shall eat of the fat of the land
19 You yourself have been commanded
Do this, take for yourselves from the land of Egypt
carts for your small ones and for your women
you shall bear away your father and come!
20 Let not your eye regret your things
for the best of all the land of Egypt shall be yours

21 The sons of Israel did so
Joseph gave them carts by order of Pharaoh
he gave them provisions for the road
22 To each and all of them he gave a change of tunics
But to Benjamin he gave three hundred silver-pieces
and five changes of tunics
23 To his father he sent this
ten asses bearing Egypt's best
ten she-asses bearing grain
and bread and victuals for his father for the road
24 He sent his brothers off and they went
He said to them, Do not fret on the road!

25 They went up from Egypt
and came to the land of Canaan, to their father Jacob
26 They told him, saying, Joseph is still alive!
Yes, he is ruler over all the land of Egypt!
His heart grew numb
for he did not trust them
27 They spoke to him all Joseph's words
that he had spoken to them

He saw the carts Joseph had sent to bear him
Then their father Jacob's breath came alive
28   and Israel said, Enough! My son Joseph is still alive!
I will go and see him before I die

CHAPTER 46

1   Israel set out with all he had and came to Beer-sheba
    He sacrificed sacrifices
    to the Elohim of his father Isaac

2   Elohim said to Israel in visions of the night
    he said, Jacob! Jacob!
    He said, Here I am
3   He said, I, the El, the Elohim of your father!
    Do not be afraid to go down to Egypt
    for I will set you up as a great nation there
4   I myself will go down with you to Egypt
    and up! I myself will also bring you up
    and Joseph shall put his hand on your eyes

5   Jacob rose up from Beer-sheba
    The sons of Israel bore away their father Jacob
    their small ones and their women
    in the carts that Pharaoh had sent to bear him
6   They took their live-stock
    their gain they had gained in the land of Canaan
    and came to Egypt
    Jacob and all his seed with him
7   His sons and his sons' sons with him
    his daughters and his sons' daughters, all his seed
    he brought with him to Egypt

8   These are the names of the sons of Israel
    who came to Egypt, Jacob and his sons

    Jacob's first-born Reuben
9   Reuben's sons

Hanoch, Pallu, Hezron and Carmi
10   Simeon's sons
Jemuel, Jamin, Ohad
Jachin, Zohar and Shaul son of the Canaanite woman
11   Levi's sons
Gershon, Kohath and Merari
12   Judah's sons
Er, Onan, Shelah, Perez and Zerah
—but Er had died with Onan in the land of Canaan—
The sons of Perez were Hezron and Hamul
13   Issachar's sons
Tola, Puvah, Job and Shimron
14   Zebulun's sons
Sered, Elon and Jahleel
15   These are the sons of Leah
that she bred for Jacob in Paddan-aram
and his daughter Dinah
All the souls, his sons and his daughters—33

16   Gad's sons
Ziphion, Haggi, Shuni, Ezbon
Eri, Arodi and Areli
17   Asher's sons
Imnah, Ishvah, Ishvi
Beriah and their sister Serah
The sons of Beriah, Heber and Malchiel
18   These are the sons of Zilpah
whom Laban had given to his daughter Leah
These she bred for Jacob—16 souls

19   The sons of Jacob's woman Rachel
Joseph and Benjamin
20   Bred for Joseph in the land of Egypt

bred for him by Asenath
daughter of Poti-phera, priest of On
Manasseh and Ephraim
21 Benjamin's sons
Bela, Becher, Ashbel
Gera, Naaman, Ehi, Rosh
Muppim, Huppim and Ard
22 These are the sons of Rachel, bred for Jacob
all the souls—14

23 Dan's son, Hushim
24 Naphtali's sons
Jahzeel, Guni, Jezer and Shillem
25 These are the sons of Bilhah
whom Laban had given to his daughter Rachel
These she bred for Jacob
all the souls—7

26 All the souls who came with Jacob to Egypt
issued from his thighs
apart from the women of Jacob's sons
all the souls—66
27 Joseph's sons, bred for him in Egypt
souls—2
All the souls of the house of Jacob
that came to Egypt—70

28 He had sent Judah on before him to Joseph
to lead on before him to Goshen
They came to the land of Goshen
29 Joseph hitched up his chariot
and went up to Goshen to greet his father Israel

He was seen by him, he fell on his neck
and wept on his neck again and again
30 Israel said to Joseph, I can die this time
after seeing your face
yes, you are still alive!

31 Joseph said to his brothers
and to his father's household
I will go up and tell Pharaoh and say to him
My brothers and my father's household
who were in the land of Canaan
have come to me!
32 The men are shepherds of flocks
yes, they are live-stock men
Their flocks, their herds and all that is theirs
they have brought
33 When Pharaoh calls you and says
What do you do?
34 you shall say, Your servants have been live-stock men
from our boyhood until now
we and our fathers also
so shall you settle in the land of Goshen
for all shepherds of flocks are an abhorrence to Egypt

CHAPTER 47

1 Joseph came and told Pharaoh, he said
   My father and my brothers, their flocks, their herds
   and all that is theirs
   have come from the land of Canaan
   Here they are in the land of Goshen!
2 From among his brothers he had taken five men
   and presented them before Pharaoh
3 Pharaoh said to his brothers, What do you do?
   They said to Pharaoh
   Your servants are shepherds of flocks
   we and our fathers also
4 They said to Pharaoh
   We have come to sojourn in the land
   for there is no pasture for your servants' flocks
   for the hunger is heavy in the land of Canaan
   Now please let your servants settle in the land of Goshen
5 Pharaoh said to Joseph
   Your father and your brothers have come to you
6 The land of Egypt is before you
   In the best of the land
   settle your father and your brothers
   let them settle in the land of Goshen
   And if you know that there are capable men among them
   set them as chiefs of live-stock over what is mine

7 Joseph brought his father Jacob

205

and had him stand him before Pharaoh
Jacob blessed Pharaoh
8   Pharaoh said to Jacob
How many days are the years of your life?
9   Jacob said to Pharaoh
The days of the years of my sojourning are 130 years
Few and full of harm
the days of the years of my life have been!
They have not attained the days of the years
of my fathers' lives in the days of their sojourning!
10   Jacob blessed Pharaoh
He went out from before Pharaoh
11   Joseph settled his father and his brothers
and gave them property in the land of Egypt
in the best of the land, in the land of Rameses
as Pharaoh had commanded
12   Joseph maintained his father, his brothers
and all his father's household
with bread, down to the small ones

13   There was no bread on all the earth
for the hunger was very heavy
The land of Egypt and the land of Canaan
were exhausted because of the hunger
14   Joseph gleaned all the silver
to be found in the land of Egypt
and in the land of Canaan
in exchange for the supplies that were supplied
Joseph brought the silver into Pharaoh's house
15   The silver was spent in the land of Egypt
and in the land of Canaan
and all Egypt came to Joseph, saying
Come! Bread for us!

Why let us die opposite you
for the silver has come to an end!

16 Joseph said, Come! Your live-stock!
I will give to you for your live-stock
if the silver has come to an end

17 They brought their live-stock to Joseph
Joseph gave them bread for the horses
the stock of sheep, the stock of oxen and the asses
He tended them with bread
in exchange for all their live-stock that year

18 That year was spent
They came to him the second year
and said to him, We will not mask from my lord
that if the silver is spent
and the stock of cattle is my lord's
nothing remains for my lord but our bodies and our ground

19 Why let us die before your eyes, ourselves and our ground
Acquire us and our ground for bread   [also?
We and our ground will be Pharaoh's servants
But give seed
we will live and not die
and the ground will not be desolate

20 Joseph acquired all Egypt's ground for Pharaoh
for each man in Egypt sold his field
for the hunger had a grip on them
The land became Pharaoh's

21 He made the people pass, whole townships
from one end of Egypt's territory to its other end

22 Only the priests' ground he did not acquire
for it was Pharaoh's law for the priests

21 whole townships: Hebrew obscure.

they ate from their allotment
that Pharaoh had given them
So they did not sell their ground

23   Joseph said to the people
Here, I have acquired you today
along with your ground for Pharaoh
Here is seed for you, seed the ground!

24   When the crops come in
you shall give a fifth to Pharaoh
Four handfuls shall be yours
as seed of the field
as food for you and for those in your households
and as food for your small ones

25   They said, You have kept us alive!
We will find favour in my lord's eyes
Let us be Pharaoh's servants!

26   Joseph set it up as a law until this day
concerning Egypt's ground, a fifth for Pharaoh
Only the priests' ground that alone
did not become Pharaoh's

27   Israel settled in the land of Egypt
in the land of Goshen
They acquired property in it
They were fruitful and increased much

28   Jacob lived in the land of Egypt for seventeen years
Jacob's days, the years of his life were 147 years

29   Israel's days drew near to death
He called his son Joseph and said to him
Please if I have found favour in your eyes
please set your hand under my thigh

do me kindness and truth
please do not entomb me in Egypt
30   When I lie down with my fathers
bear me away from Egypt, entomb me in their tomb
He said, I will do according to your word
31   He said, Swear to me!
He swore to him
Israel prostrated himself at the head of the bed

CHAPTER 48

1   After these things, they said to Joseph
    Here, your father is sick!
    He took his two sons with him, Manasseh and Ephraim
2   They told Jacob and said
    Here, your son Joseph has come to you
    Israel took a grip on himself and sat up on the bed

3   Jacob said to Joseph, El Shaddai was seen by me at Luz
    in the land of Canaan
    He blessed me
4   He said to me
    Here, I will make you fruitful and increase you
    I will give you to be an assembly of peoples
    I will give this land to your seed after you
    as everlasting property!
5   Now, your two sons bred for you in the land of Egypt
    before I came to you in Egypt
    let them be mine
    Ephraim and Manasseh
    like Reuben and Simeon, shall be mine
6   Your children that you bred after them
    let them be yours
    By their brothers' names they shall be called
    regarding their inheritance
7   I—
    when I was coming from Paddan, Rachel died on me
    in the land of Canaan on the road
    still a stretch of land from Ephrath

I entombed her there on the road to Ephrath
—that is Bethlehem

8   Israel saw Joseph's sons and said
Who are these?

9   Joseph said to his father
They are my sons whom Elohim has given me here
He said, Please bring them to me
and I will bless them

10   Israel's eyes were heavy with age
He was not able to see
He drew them close to him
kissed them and embraced them

11   Israel said to Joseph
I did not presume I would see your face!
And here, Elohim has let me see your seed also!

12   Joseph brought them out from between his knees
and prostrated himself, his face to the earth

13   Joseph took the two of them
Ephraim with his right hand, to Israel's left
Manasseh with his left hand, to Israel's right
and he brought them close to him

14   But Israel put out his right and set it on Ephraim's head
—he was the younger!—
and his left on Manasseh's head
crossing his hands
for Manasseh was the first-born

15   He blessed Joseph and said
The Elohim before whose face my fathers walked
Abraham and Isaac
the Elohim who has been my shepherd my life long
until this day

16   the messenger who has redeemed me from all harm
      bless the boys!
      Let my name be called through them
      and the name of my fathers Abraham and Isaac
      They shall teem abundant in the land's inwards
17 Joseph saw that his father had put his right hand
    on Ephraim's head
    It was bad in his eyes
    He took hold of his father's hand to turn it aside
    from Ephraim's head to Manasseh's head
18 Joseph said to his father, Not so, my father
    for this one is the first-born
    Set your right on his head!
19 But his father refused and said, I know, my son, I know
    He too shall become a people
    He too shall be great
    Nevertheless, his younger brother shall be greater than he
    and his seed shall become fullness of nations!
20 He blessed them on that day, saying
          Through you shall Israel bless, saying
          Elohim set you up like Ephraim and like Manasseh!
    He put Ephraim before Manasseh

21 Israel said to Joseph, Here, I am dying
    but Elohim will be with you
    He will make you return to the land of your fathers
22 Myself I give you
    one shoulder (Shechem) more than your brothers
    which I took from the hand of the Amorite
    with my sword and my bow

CHAPTER 49

1 Jacob called his sons and said
      Gather! I will tell you
      what will happen to you in the after-days
2   Collect! Hear, sons of Jacob
      hear your father Israel

3   Reuben, my first-born, you
      my force, firstling of my virility
      excelling in loftiness
      excelling in vigour!
4   Turbulent as water, you shall excel no more
      for you went up to your father's couch
      then you profaned my sheets by going up!

5   Simeon and Levi, brothers!
      vessels of violence, their tools!
6   Come not into their secret, my soul!
      Unite not with their assembly, my honour!
      For in their anger they have killed a man
      and at their pleasure have maimed a bull
7   Cursed their anger so fierce
      their fury so harsh!
      I will disperse them in Jacob
      I will scatter them in Israel

8   Judah, you, your brothers shall laud you
      your hand on your enemies' nape!
      Your father's sons shall lie prostrate before you

9 Whelp of a lion, Judah
from torn prey, my son, you come up!
He bends, he crouches like a lion
like a great cat Who shall rouse him?

10 The rod shall not turn aside from Judah
nor the sceptre from between his feet
until Shilo comes
His the obedience of peoples!

11 He tethers his ass-colt to the vine
his ass's young to the vinestock
In wine he washes his clothes
his cape in the blood of grapes

12 His eyes more crimson than wine
his teeth whiter than milk

13 Zebulun by the sea-shore shall dwell
Let him be a shore for ships
his flank against Sidon!

14 Issachar a strong-boned ass
crouched between the pens

15 he saw a resting-place How good!
and the land How pleasant!
He bowed his shoulder to carry
and became a task-work serf

16 Dan shall judge his people
as one of the rods of Israel

17 Dan shall be a serpent on the road
a viper by the way

10 until Shilo comes: Hebrew obscure.

biting the horse's heels
Backwards falls its rider!

18   I hope for your salvation, YHWH!

19   Gad, the raiders shall raid him
but he shall raid on their heels

20   Of Asher rich is his bread
he shall give king's delights
21   Naphtali a fleet hind
giving comely fawns

22   Young of a wild ass, Joseph
young of a wild ass by a pool
onagers above a wall
23   They harried him and shot at him
They bore him malice, the archers!
24   But his bow stayed steady
his arms, his hands agile
by the hands of the Leader of Jacob
there, the Shepherd, the Stone of Israel
25   By your father's El—he shall help you
with Shaddai—he shall bless you!
Blessings of skies above
blessings of the deep that crouches below
blessings of nipples and womb!
26   Your father's blessings
are mightier than the blessings of mountains eternal
the allurements of the everlasting hills

22 Meaning of verse uncertain.
26 First half of verse: Hebrew uncertain.

> They shall be upon Joseph's head
> on the crown of one singled out from his brothers

27 Benjamin a wolf that tears
   in the morning he eats quarry
   in the evening he shares plunder

28 All these, the rods of Israel, twelve
   Thus their father spoke to them
   He blessed them
   each according to his blessing, he blessed them
29 He commanded them and said to them
   I am to be gathered to my people
   Entomb me with my fathers
   in the cave which is in the field of Ephron the Hittite
30 in the cave which is in the field of Machpelah
   which faces Mamre in the land of Canaan
   the field that Abraham acquired
   from Ephron the Hittite for entombment property
31 There they entombed Abraham and his woman Sarah
   There they entombed Isaac and his woman Rebekah
   There I entombed Leah
32 An acquisition the field and the cave in it
   from the Sons of Heth

33 Jacob had finished his commands to his sons
   He gathered his feet into the bed
   passed away and was gathered to his people

CHAPTER 50

1 Joseph fell upon his father's face
wept over him and kissed him

2 Joseph commanded his servants the healers
to embalm his father
The healers embalmed Israel

3 Forty days were fulfilled for him
for thus the days of embalming are fulfilled
The Egyptians wept for him seventy days

4 The days of weeping for him passed
Joseph spoke to Pharaoh's household, saying
Please if I have found favour in your eyes
please speak in Pharaoh's ears, saying

5 My father made me swear, saying
Here, I am dying
In my tomb that I hollowed out for myself
in the land of Canaan
you shall entomb me!
Now, please let me go up and entomb my father
and I will return!

6 Pharaoh said, Go up and entomb your father
as he made you swear

7 Joseph went up to entomb his father
Went up with him all Pharaoh's servants
the elders of his household
and all the elders of the land of Egypt

8 all Joseph's household

his brothers and his father's household
Only their small ones, their flocks and their herds
they left in the land of Goshen

9   Went up with him chariots also and horsemen also
It was a very heavy camp

10   They came to Goren-ha-Atad
which is beyond the Jordan
They wailed there a great and very heavy wailing
He made for his father a mourning of seven days

11   The settler of the land, the Canaanite saw the mourning
at Goren-ha-Atad
They said, This is a heavy mourning for Egypt!
So they called its name Mourning of Egypt (Abel-mizraim)
which is beyond the Jordan

12   His sons did for him as he had commanded them

13   His sons bore him to the land of Canaan
They entombed him
in the cave of the field of Machpelah
the field that Abraham had acquired
for entombment property
from Ephron the Hittite, facing Mamre

14   Joseph returned to Egypt, he, his brothers
and all who had gone up with him to entomb his father
after he had entombed his father

15   Joseph's brothers saw that their father was dead
They said, What if Joseph bears us malice!
Return! he will return us all the harm
that we rendered him

16   They commanded Joseph, saying

Your father commanded before his death, saying

17   Thus shall you say to Joseph
Ah, please bear your brothers' fault and their sin
for they rendered you harm!
Now, please bear
the fault of the servants of your father's Elohim!
Joseph wept when they spoke to him

18   His brothers themselves went, fell down before him
and said, Here we are, your servants!

19   Joseph said to them, Do not be afraid!
For am I in the place of Elohim?

20   You, you thought up harm against me
Elohim thought it for good
in order to do as on this day
to keep many people alive

21   Now, do not be afraid!
I myself will maintain you and your small ones!
He comforted them and spoke to their hearts

22   Joseph settled in Egypt, he and his father's household
Joseph lived 110 years

23   Joseph saw the third generation of Ephraim's sons
The sons of Machir son of Manasseh
were also bred on Joseph's knees

24   Joseph said to his brothers, I am dying
Elohim will take charge! he will take charge of you
and bring you up from this land
to the land that he swore
to Abraham, to Isaac and to Jacob

25   Joseph made the sons of Israel swear, saying

Elohim will take charge! he will take charge of you
and you shall bring my bones up from here!

26   Joseph died at 110 years of age
       They embalmed him and set him in a coffin in Egypt

TRANSLATOR'S POSTSCRIPT

AT THE START: GENESIS MADE NEW

This translation of the Hebrew text of Genesis has absorbed the better part of nine years. During that period I never for a moment wearied of the task I had undertaken: to produce a new English version that would reflect the original as faithfully as possible.

The method of work I have adopted is indirectly inherited from Martin Buber and Franz Rosenzweig (*Im Anfang*, 1930). These German translators were followed, among others, by the French-speaking translators Edmond Fleg (*Le Livre du Commencement*, 1946) and André Chouraqui (*L'Univers de la Bible*, 1982). These translators were innovative in various ways but perhaps the most interesting thing they did was to reflect each Hebrew word by one and the same word in the target language, repeating the word wherever it is repeated in the original text and choosing paronyms to show how words in the same etymological group are related to one another.

This may seem a technical point but it is an important one, as it enables the reader to perceive patterns and associations in the text that remain hidden in other translations. The new patterns, which are really old patterns, challenge certain accepted interpretations of the Genesis text that have influenced our various cultures. I will illustrate this, in the coming paragraphs, by commenting on words from the story of the Garden of Eden. This story has greatly influenced the concept of the status of women in society. Other words lend themselves to an ecological interpretation.

The Hebrew text

At the Start: Genesis Made New is not based on a special study of Hebrew manuscripts. The Hebrew text used is the *Biblia Hebraica Stuttgartensia* (1967–77). Produced by German scholars, who revised and perfected an earlier edition by Kittel (1929), the "B.H.S." has won universal recognition in academic circles.

At the Start . . .

The book that is called *Genesis* in English is known as *Bereshit* in Hebrew. *Bereshit* is traditionally translated as "In the beginning" and, in this version, as "At the start." *Bereshit* is the first word of the first book of the Bible. In Hebrew tradition, the first word or phrase of a book is also its title.

But why "start" rather than "beginning"? Thought has been given to this choice. "Start" suggests an initial impulse that sets all things in motion. It covers a space as well as a time dimension. Though unfamiliar in this context, it is nonetheless an exact rendering of *Bereshit* and, hopefully, its very unfamiliarity will be seen as an invitation to the reader to take a fresh look at this ancient text.

A "word for word" translation

At the Start: Genesis Made New is a literal, "word for word" translation. To ensure exactness, a great deal of spadework has been done at the semantic level to determine which English word can systematically correspond to a given Hebrew word. This way of treating vocabulary differs from that of traditional translators, who replace a single Hebrew word by a variety of English words for reasons of style or context. Some examples will clarify what is meant here.

amar, "to say"

A first, simple example. In Genesis 18,17–33, the verb *amar,* "to say," is repeated thirteen times. The eminent scholar Ephraim Speiser (*Genesis,* 1962) translates the verb *amar* in this passage by seven different locutions: "to say, to reply, to reflect, to speak up, to persist, to answer," and "came the reply." Speiser may be said to improve on the original for stylistic reasons. In fact, the Hebrew language does not possess this extensive range of words to introduce direct speech. It has one word, *amar.* In the present version, *amar* is rendered exactly by "to say."

sela, "rib" or "side"?

A second example illustrates how traditional translators choose different English words to fit particular contexts. The noun *sela* is commonly translated as "side." It means "side" as in "hillside" or as in the "side of the tabernacle." In the passage describing the creation of woman (Gn 2, 21–22), however, the word "rib" is usually adopted for *sela,* hence the expression "Adam's rib." In *At the Start: Genesis Made New, sela* is consistently translated as "side":

> He took one of its sides
> and closed up the flesh in its place
> YHWH Elohim built the side
> he had taken from the groundling into woman (Gn 2,21–22)

It may seem daring, but is is logical, to replace the traditional "rib" by the word "side" here. This decision is well supported, moreover, by a secular tradition: a substantial number of rabbinical commentaries infer that woman was built from a human "side." The same teaching then concludes that woman begins where man ends, she is his limit, and vice versa. Theirs is a "side by side" relationship.

The expression "bone from my bone, flesh from my flesh" (Gn 2,23), which follow the creation of woman, may have contributed to the interpretation "Adam's rib." They merely emphasize, however, the closeness of the man-woman relationship: Jacob's uncle Laban uses similar words when claiming kinship with his nephew in Genesis 29,14.

''To breed'' and ''breedings''

In some rare cases, the systematic adoption of one and the same word in the target language involves an adaptation of English to Hebrew usage. By way of an example, I will take the verb *yalad*, which I have translated by "to breed." In Hebrew, *yalad* is used for men, women, and animals. I therefore looked for a general term in English, hoping to encourage the reader to reflect on the insight to be gained from having a common word for human and animal reproduction. Most of the words currently used in English Bibles had to be rejected, because they are too specific. There is the consecrated biblical term "to beget" for a male parent, "to bear, to bring forth, to give birth" for a female parent, and "to bring forth," "to drop," or "to breed" for animals. For my purpose, the last verb quoted is the only feasible one.

Is anything gained by a "word for word" rendering here? I suggest that the use of a single verb for humans and animals implies kinship between the species. This closeness to animals and respect for animal life is confirmed in other ways in the text. Genesis 2,19–20, for instance, describes how *YHWH Elohim* makes bird and beast as potential companions for the human being, who in turn establishes relationship with them by giving them names. Again, before the flood, humans are strictly vegetarian. Only after the flood is mankind allowed to kill for food (Gn 9,3) and then under conditions that are strictly regulated (Gn 9,4). There could be a lesson here for modern society: it is hardly necessary to point out the disastrous effects of human indifference and cruelty with regard to the exploitation of certain animal species today.

To return to the technicalities of translation, besides establishing a one-to-one connection at lexical level, *At the Start: Genesis Made New* also echoes Hebrew paronyms. The noun *toldedot* is formed from the same root as the above-mentioned verb yalad. Toledot is usually translated as "story" or "history," when it refers to the creation of the skies and the earth (Gn 2,4), and by "generations" in the case of human genealogies (Gn 5,1; 6,9; 10,1–32 . . .). Because of this difference of vocabulary, the connection that exists in Hebrew between the creation of the universe and human procreation is habitually lost. I have translated *toledot* by "breedings":

> These are the breedings of the skies and the earth
> at their creation (Gn 2,4)

> This is the record of the breedings of Adam (Gn 5,1)

The breedings of Noah, the breedings of the sons of Noah, the breedings of Shem, of Terah, of Ishmael, of Esau, of Jacob! A single root links animal life, human life, and the life of the universe. Through these cross-connections the whole of creation and the whole of human history are seen to be united in a single process of birth. This biblical metaphor is rich. It conveys a respect for life and compares favorably with the crudely technical "big bang."

adam, "groundling" and *adamah*, "ground"

Another example of paronyms is provided by the words *adam* and *adamah*. In the first five chapters of Genesis *adam* and *adamah* are key words: *adam* occurs twenty-nine times, *adamah* sixteen times. In the following passage, the Hebrew words have been retained:

> and there was no *adam* to serve the *adamah*
> But a surge went up from the earth
> and gave drink to all the face of the *adamah*
> YHWH Elohim formed the *adam,* soil of the *adamah*
> He blew into its nostrils the blast of life
> and the *adam* became a living soul
> YHWH Elohim planted a garden in Eden to the east
> There he set the *adam* he had formed
> YHWH Elohim made sprout from the *adamah*
> all trees attractive to see and good for eating (Gn 2,5–9)

In this quotation, the etymological link between *adam* and *adamah* is emphasized by repetition. The link is meaningful. To render it significantly in English, I have translated *adam* as "groundling" and *adamah* as "ground." By contrast, in the Revised Standard Version (ed. 1973), Genesis 2,5 reads "there was no man to till the ground" and Genesis 2,7 as "the Lord God formed man of dust from the ground." The Hebrew link between "man" and "ground" is lost here.

The repetitive pattern observed in Genesis 2,5–9 provides an infrastructure that sustains two important concepts: line 1 suggests that even before it was created, the destiny of the "groundling" was to serve the "ground"; in line 4 there is a hint of mother-earth (*adamah* is feminine), from which the "groundling" is formed, like the trees (Gn 2,9), the animals and the birds (Gn 2,19). These observations add nuance to the well-established view that Man was made to dominate the earth!

In traditional versions, two Hebrew words, *adam* and *ish,* are translated by one English word, "man." This leads to confusion. In the new version, "man" is reserved for *ish.* This latter choice will be discussed below. In the meantime, an attentive reading of the first account of creation reveals that *adam* was not a man:

> *Elohim* said
> *We will make* a groundling (*adam*)

in our image, after *our* likeness
Let them govern the fish of the sea
the fowl of the skies, the cattle, all the earth
every creeper that creeps on the earth
Elohim created the groundling in his image
created it in the image of *Elohim*
male and female created *them*
Elohim blessed *them*
Elohim said to *them*
Be fruitful, increase, fill the earth, *subject* it (1,26–28)

The plural words in this passage are in italic characters. The groundling, *adam*, appears as a plural being, made in the image of a plural God; the Hebrew name for God, *Elohim*, has a plural ending. The "them" that refers to *adam* reflects the "we" that refers to *Elohim*. It is true that the way the Hebrew language switches from plural to singular is disconcerting, (the verb "created" and the pronoun "his" are in the singular), but this should not mask the Hebrew perception of *adam* as a creature with a twofold aspect. The nature of *adam*'s plurality is clearly stated here: *adam* is male and female. "Be fruitful, increase, fill . . ." are plural imperatives. The command to "be fruitful" can only be carried out by male and female together.

Biblical commentators have speculated on this text. Some claim that the original *adam* was an androgyne. One thing is sure: *adam* here is not a male. English Bibles translate the eighth line of the above quotation as follows: "in the image of God created *him*" (Gn 1,27). "Him" is grammatically correct but it is an androcentric translation. Following Phyllis Trible (*God and the Rhetoric of Sexuality*, 1978), I have preferred the neutral pronoun "it," which may refer to the androgyne or may refer to the human couple. "It" excludes neither male nor female.

It is only later in the text that *Adam* is attributed as a proper name to the father of mankind (Gn 4,25 ff.).

ish, "man" and *ishah,* "wo-man"

Like *adam* the word *ish* is one of a pair, *ish* and *ishah*. Although *ish* and *ishah* are not etymologically related, they are linked by a common sound. Such sound associations found popular etymology. They too are significant. *Ish* and *ishah* have one syllable in common and one odd syllable. At language level, the common syllable expresses similarity, the odd syllable reflects difference. These subtleties are well rendered in English by "man" and "wo-man."

> YHWH Elohim built the side
> he had taken from the groundling into woman
> He brought her to the groundling
> The groundling said
> > This one this time
> > is bone from my bone
> > flesh from my flesh
> > This one shall be called wo-man
> > for from man
> > she has been taken this one (Gn 2,22–23)

It has traditionally been concluded that priority belongs to man, as he is created first: woman is an offshoot of man, formed from his body, built from a "rib."

Careful examination of the text refutes this interpretation. The word "man," *ish,* appears in the text for the first time in Genesis 2,23, after the appearance of "woman," *ishah* (Gn 2,22). The "groundling," which was two-in-one in the first chapter (Gn 1,26–28), is now separated into two entities. The suggestion is that when "woman" is taken from "the groundling," "man" remains. He is, because she is, and vice versa. This act of separation harmonizes with the description of creation in the first chapter, when *Elohim* separates the light from the darkness, earth from seas, and day from night (Gn 1,4.9.19).

Naming

Popular etymology plays an important role in the Hebrew text when names are given. A new name is often followed by a sentence justifying its attribution. The name is linked to what follows by a common sound. It is virtually impossible to transfer this repetition of sounds to the target language. I have only succeeded once:

> She called his name *Seth*
> "for Elohim has *set* another seed in Abel's place . . . (4,25)

The kind of word play represented by "Seth" and "set" is usually either ignored or explained in a footnote.

The name "Eve"

In Genesis 3,20, the name *Hawwa*, "Eve," occurs for the first time. If the Hebrew words are maintained in the text, it is obvious where the word play lies:

> The groundling called his woman's name *Hawwa*
> for she is the mother of all *hay* (3,20)

In *At the Start: Genesis Made New*, to ensure that the justification of the name is read with correct emphasis, the name is translated by the corresponding English word. *Hawwa* means "life" or "living."

> The groundling called his woman's name *Life* (Eve)
> for she is the mother of all that lives (3,20)

The familiar English name follows in parentheses and subsequently this name is used in the traditional manner:

The groundling knew his woman Eve (4,1)

In the Revised Standard Version (ed. 1973), verse 3,20 reads as follows: "The man called his wife's name Eve because she was the mother of all living." A comment: "The name in Hebrew resembles the word for living" is added in a footnote. The expression "all living" seems vague: one hesitates over its meaning. Ronald Knox (*Genesis,* 1955) is more precise: "The name which Adam gave his wife was Eve, Life, because she was the mother of all living men." In both cases, however, as in other English Bibles, the reader understands that the woman receives the name Eve because she is the "mother of mankind."

Motherhood is not the main point of the Hebrew verse. The main point is the connection between Eve's name and "life." Eve has been sufficiently accused of bringing death into the world for it to be worth stopping for a moment to ponder why, when the human couple is expelled from the garden, Eve's partner gives her the name "Life." In fact, her name harks back to the mysterious tree that is described as standing in the middle of the garden of Eden. This tree has two aspects: it is the tree of "life," *es hahayim,* and the tree of the knowing of good and bad (Gn 2,9). When the woman takes the fruit of the tree in the middle of the garden (Gn 3,3.6.), she becomes life's channel, bringing within the sphere of human experience all that life represents for good and bad. The gift of life is necessarily attended by its concomitant, death. Only secondarily, but very suitably, can Eve be called the "mother of mankind."

"Pains" and "pains"

The balance and harmony that characterize the relationship of newly created man and woman in the Hebrew text have often been obscured in translation. Here is a final example. In the following passage, I have translated the words *issabon* and *eseb* by "pains."

> To the woman he said
> Increase! I will increase
> your pains (*issabon*) and your conceivings
> With pains (*eseb*) you shall breed sons (3,16)

> To the groundling he said . . .
> cursed is the ground for you
> With pains (*issabon*) you shall eat of it
> all the days of your life (3,17)

Prestigious translations here emphasize woman's suffering and man's achievement. The influence of the Greek Septuagint: "I will greatly multiply thy pains and thy moanings" (Gn 3,16) is apparent, for instance, in the New English Bible (ed. 1970):

> To the woman he said,
> I will increase your labor and your *groaning*
> and in labor you shall bear children (3,16)

> And to the man he said,
> With labor you shall *win* your food from it (3,17)

> You shall *gain* your bread by the sweat of your brow (3,19)

Where the New English Bible has the verbs "win" and "gain," the Hebrew text simply has, in both cases, "you shall eat." There is a touch of the subhuman here in the words addressed to woman and a hint of superman in the words addressed to man.

In fact, the Hebrew text establishes a parallel between the "pains" of woman and the "pains" of man. Both will be fruitful: by stint of effortful labor, she will produce sons and he will produce food. Internal textual evidence, a study beyond the scope of this postscript, shows that despite the labor, the results of both activities are positive.

HEBREW NAMES FOR GOD

In *At the Start: Genesis Made New* divine names are transliterated, not translated. The main ones are *Elohim, YHWH, El,* and *Shaddai.*

The noun *Elohim* means "God." *Elohim* has a plural ending. When denoting the God of the Hebrews, it is sometimes, though rarely, followed by the verb in the third person plural (Gn 20,13; 31,53; 35,7). Normally, however, it takes the verb in the third person singular, masculine form. *Elohim* is also used of foreign "gods."

YHWH, the tetragrammaton, is written without vowel sounds in the Hebrew text. The four Hebrew consonants of the tetragrammaton are connected with the verb *haya,* "to live." To manifest respect for the transcendent nature of this name, in the Hebrew-Jewish tradition this name is not pronounced. It is replaced by the reading, *Adonai,* meaning "My Lord." The vowels of *Adonai* have been inserted among the Hebrew consonants of the tetragrammaton to indicate the name's unpronounceable character. This has given rise to a further reading, "Jehovah."

El is the most ancient Semitic name for God. The word *el* means "power." In Genesis 31,29, the *el,* "power," of Laban's hand is opposed to the *Elohim* of Jacob's father. *El* is found in combined forms, such as: *El*

Elyon (God Most High), *El Olam* (God Everlasting), *El Roi* (God of Seeing). It is juxtaposed to *Shaddai* in *El Shaddai*.

Shaddai: there is no satisfactory explanation of this name. It is variously connected with the Hebrew words for "hill," "breast," or "nipple." It always occurs in a context of fertility. The customary translation "God Almighty" is partly attributed to the influence of Greek versions, partly to midrashic interpretations.

THE LAYOUT OF THE TEXT

Something must now be said about the layout of the text, for which I have had no direct models. The Hebrew text goes back to spoken origins: for centuries it had been learned by heart, recited, listened to. *At the Start: Genesis Made New* attempts to reflect this oral tradition by capturing the rhythms of the spoken text. Hebrew thought progresses step by step and even narrative texts have an inherent structure. The layout proposed here is based on the pattern that emerged from listening to a reading of the Hebrew text by Abraham Abouna (Jerusalem). It was possible to confirm the rhythms of this recited version by referring to the conjunctive and disjunctive accents as noted in the Hebrew Bible (B.H.S.). Traditional verses were thus broken down, line by line, into a pattern that looks more like verse than prose.

The new layout respects the word order of Hebrew as much as possible. Repetitions of phrases and sentences are maintained. They serve as a mnemonic. In the narrative parts, they titillate the expectancy of the reader (or listener) in a way that is characteristic of popular story-telling. Where content of message, structure, and layout correspond, repetition also draws attention to significant detail, as, for example, in the two following passages, where Joseph interprets the dreams of the chief butler and chief baker:

> This is its interpretation
> The three tendrils? They are three days
> Within three days
> Pharaoh will lift up your head
> and return you to your office (Gn 40,12–13)

> This is its interpretation
> The three baskets? They are three days
> Within three days
> Pharaoh will lift up your head off you
> and hang you on a tree (Gn 40,18–19)

FOOTNOTES

The text of *At the Start: Genesis Made New* is purposely presented without explanatory footnotes. Such notes are often helpful but they can be pernicious. They are proposed to and imposed on the reader and risk acting as a barrier between reader and text.

From its place at the roots of our culture, despite the passing of three millenniums, the first book of the Bible speaks directly to the world of today. When we look back in a historical perspective, we think of it as an old book and so it is. Yet, there is a sense in which it is a young book: the Eden myth, in particular, expresses a vision of life that is suggestive of a time when humanity first emerged from the animal world and awoke to consciousness. The power of these early myths and stories is astonishing: they have never ceased to inspire art, literature, and moral teachings; they have found expression in popular sayings, in the past, and continue to do so in the media of the present day.

The years spent in the company of this text have taught me to appre-

ciate its value. I have wept over the beauty of passages from the episode of
the deluge, delighted in the intrigues of Rebekah, shared Jacob's struggle
for independence, admired the character study of Joseph as he develops
from a priggish adolescent into a wise governor and generous brother.
This is a book about people. It is also about peoples. The Hebrew world
knew violence, wars, famine . . . And God in all that? It is striking how
the presence of *Elohim,* which is all-pervading in the first chapter, becomes more and more discreet as the stories unfold. In the Joseph cycle,
which closes the book, divine power is manifest in the wisdom that can
interpret dreams. The "breath of Elohim" that hovered over the primor-
dial waters (Gn 1,2) is present in Joseph (Gn 41,38), the man who feeds a
hungry world.

ABOUT THE TRANSLATOR

Mary Phil Korsak was born and educated in England. Her love of English literature, especially poetry, blossomed in a home among the Derbyshire moors, where words exercised endless fascination and books were the main source of entertainment. She later studied at Paris and Oxford Universities (MA modern languages). After her marriage to Léonid Korsak, she taught for many years at the Institut Supérieur des Traducteurs et Interprètes in Brussels, where she trained adult students in translation skills. She interrupted her teaching career to pursue biblical studies with Jewish and Christian teachers and has contributed articles in this field to academic and other reviews. Mary Phil and her husband live in Brussels. They have four sons and two daughters.